SHELLFISH

THE COOKBOOK

edited by
KAREN BARNABY

whitecap

First printing, 2008

Edited by Taryn Boyd
Proofread by Dianne Fowlie
Cover and interior design by Jacqui Thomas
Typeset by Setareh Ashrafologhalai
Cover and food photography by Tracey Kusiewicz, unless otherwise noted
Food styling by Irene McGuinness, unless otherwise noted
Illustrations by Heather Horton
Kitchen/tablewares provided by The Gourmet Warehouse

Printed and bound in Canada by Friesens

LIBRARY AND ARCHIVES CANADA CATALOGUING IN PUBLICATION

Shellfish : the cookbook / Karen Barnaby, editor.

Includes index.
ISBN 978-1-55285-925-4

1. Cookery (Shellfish). I. Barnaby, Karen

TX753.S54 2008   641.6'94   C2007-905569-9

The publisher acknowledges the financial support of the Government of Canada through the Book Publishing Industry Development Program (BPIDP) and the Province of British Columbia through the Book Publishing Tax Credit.

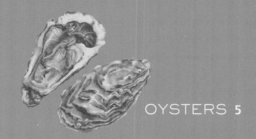

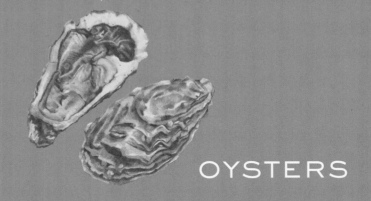

OYSTERS

The oyster's a confusing suitor

It's masc., and fem., and even neuter.

But whether husband, pal or wife

It leads a painless sort of life.

I'd like to be an oyster, say,

In August, June, July or May.

—Ogden Nash

❧

I had never eaten
one—I may have eaten a tinned, smoked oyster—but her prose
had me believing that they were both otherworldly and of this
earth as well. A mollusk to be respected, loved, and cherished.

From her book, I knew all about Hangtown Fry, Oysters
Rockefeller, oyster loaf, and oyster stew without ever having eaten
an oyster. Fisher's description of making oyster stew—especially
the way she described using your index finger to stir a pan of
raw oysters until they become too hot to stir as the indicator that
the oysters were ready to be combined with barely simmering
milk—sent shivers up my spine. From her writing I learned that
oysters start life as male, and when a year old, become female.
And that oysters spawn in months without an "r," becoming soft
and milky in texture, and lesser in flavor.

She describes one of her fantasies: a maid would sneak an
oyster loaf to her room where she and her friends waited. Her
comments perfectly echo the way I fantasized along with her
about those oysters: "And yet . . . yet those will always be, in my
mental gastronomy, on my spiritual taste buds, the most delicious oysters I ever ate."

East and West Coast Oysters

The only oyster species native to the Pacific Northwest is the tiny
Olympia, named after a community that once thrived on oyster
cultivation in Washington's Puget Sound.

As the Olympia went into near extinction due to overfishing and pollution, other varieties of oysters were imported from Japan, including the Pacific oyster (*Crassostrea gigas*), which is the most common. This oyster appears under many names that usually relate to the area in which they're grown; for example, Chef Creek, Royal Miyagi, Pearl Bay, Fanny Bay, Beach, and Kusshi are all the same oyster. The less prevalent Kumamoto (*Crassostrea sikamea*) is another tiny oyster, well suited to novice oyster eaters.

On the East Coast of Canada, *Crassostrea virginica* is the ruling oyster. Some of the delicious names it goes by are Malpeque, Caraquet, and Tatamagouche. The Mountain Island flat oyster (*Ostrea edulis*) was introduced in the late 1950s. It is the indigenous species of Europe and commonly known as Belon. The name Belon, however, should apply only to oysters raised in Brittany, France.

Storing and Preparing Oysters

When buying live oysters, find a shop that either stores them under running water or keeps them cup side down (flat side up) on ice. Oysters that are kept in a jumble will lose juice and flavor. When buying oysters, pick them up; they should feel heavy for their size. Light oysters will have lost their juices and the meat with be thin.

To store them at home, arrange them cup side down under a damp towel. This will prevent further loss of their juices. Scrub well and rinse just before shucking. If the oysters are fresh, they'll last for five days.

There are many different ways to serve freshly shucked oysters. Some people will eat them as is, or with only the merest hint of lemon juice. Some thrive on oysters with cocktail or Tabasco sauce. Some like them served with fresh or store-bought salsa. Try steeping whole black peppercorns in vodka for a few weeks, then sprinkling the vodka over the oysters. Freshly grated horseradish is delicious, and prepared, bottled horseradish is not too bad either. Another simple sauce is sour cream with finely chopped cucumber. Mignonette sauce is a classic sauce for oysters, and is made from good wine vinegar with finely chopped shallots. Ponzu, a Japanese influenced sauce, is made from soy sauce and citrus.

Experiment with different ingredients. Just make sure that there is a little acid to balance the flavor of the oysters.

Using Pre-shucked Oysters

A lot of people don't know how to shuck oysters. Don't worry, it's not a character flaw. You can avoid all the trouble of shucking oysters by simply buying containers of pre-shucked oysters. You can find fresh or frozen pre-shucked oysters in half pints, pints, and quarts. If frozen, thaw in the fridge and eat within two days.

The oysters are sized from small to extra large, with large and extra large being the most common. The large and extra-large oysters can be cut in half for frying, stews, and chowders. As a general rule of thumb:

- Extra Large: 10–15 oysters per quart
- Large: 15–25 oysters per quart
- Medium: 26–32 oysters per quart
- Small: 33–40 oysters per quart

Mignonette Sauce

Makes ½ cup (125 mL).

You can add 2 Tbsp (30 mL) of finely diced apple to this just before serving.

½ cup	white or red wine vinegar	125 mL
2 Tbsp	finely chopped shallots	30 mL
to taste	sea salt	to taste

Mix all the ingredients and refrigerate until ready to serve.

Ponzu Sauce

Makes approximately 1 cup (250 mL).

The ingredients for this can be found in Japanese grocery stores and well-stocked Asian markets.

½ cup	mirin (sweet rice wine)	125 mL
¼ cup	rice vinegar	60 mL
2 Tbsp	soy sauce	30 mL
¼ cup	bonito flakes (shaved, dried tuna)	60 mL
2 Tbsp	fresh lemon juice, or more to taste	30 mL

Combine the mirin, vinegar, soy sauce, and bonito flakes in a small pot and bring to a boil over medium heat. Remove from the heat and let cool.

Pour the sauce through a strainer into a bowl; discard the bonito flakes. Add the lemon juice. Store in a glass jar with a tight-fitting lid in the refrigerator for up to 1 week. Add more lemon juice if needed before serving.

The inspiration for this soup came from the Portuguese soup called *caldo verde,* which uses smoked Portuguese chouriço sausage instead of the oysters. I think this version is almost as good as the original. Serves 6–8.

POTATO, KALE & OYSTER SOUP

INGREDIENTS

¼ cup	extra virgin olive oil	60 mL
3	medium onions, thinly sliced	3
2 lb	potatoes, peeled and thinly sliced (russet or Yukon Gold)	1 kg
10 cups	chicken stock or water	2.5 L
1 tsp	sea salt	5 mL
1 lb	kale, washed (stems removed)	500 g
1 quart	pre-shucked oysters with juice, cut into bite-sized pieces	1 L
to taste	freshly ground black pepper	to taste

METHOD

Heat the oil in a large pot over medium heat. Add the onions and cook until soft but not brown. Add the potatoes, chicken stock or water, and sea salt. Bring to a boil. Turn the heat down to a simmer and cook until the potatoes are very tender, about 1 hour.

In batches, purée the soup in a food processor or blender and return to the pot. Bring to a simmer. Thinly shred the kale—the thinner, the better. Add to the soup and simmer for 20 minutes.

Just before serving, add the oysters and their juice to the simmering soup and stir for a few minutes. Season with the black pepper (I like to use a lot!). Serve immediately.

Buy some fresh local oysters in the shell—not too large, as the small, plump ones are sweeter. Allow 2–3 per person. Shuck the oysters, severing the muscle that attaches the oyster to the shell, and remove any bits of shell left behind. Makes 1 cup (250 mL).

FRESH OYSTERS

ON THE HALF SHELL WITH MIGNONETTE SAUCE

INGREDIENTS

1 cup	tarragon vinegar	250 mL
2	shallots or 1 small red onion, finely chopped	2
½ tsp	lemon zest	2 mL
½ tsp	sea salt	2 mL
½ tsp	hot pepper sauce	2 mL
to taste	freshly ground black pepper	to taste
18	oysters	18

METHOD

Combine the vinegar, shallots, lemon zest, sea salt, hot pepper sauce, and black pepper and refrigerate until ready to use.

Present the oysters on a deep serving platter lined with an abundance of rosemary or other greenery. Leave a space in the middle for a small bowl of the mignonette sauce. If you are serving a lot of oysters, put ice under the greens. Let your guests spoon a little mignonette sauce on their own oysters—some purists like to slurp their oysters au naturel.

I created this recipe to use the pre-shucked oysters you can find at the seafood shop. The puréed base of potatoes, oyster mushrooms, and spinach lets you get away with using less cream than usual. Oyster stew is traditional at Christmas time—with slivers of brilliant green spinach and red bell pepper, it's particularly festive. Serves 6.

DOUBLE OYSTER & SPINACH CHOWDER

INGREDIENTS

1 Tbsp	butter	15 mL
1 Tbsp	olive oil	15 mL
1	large onion, minced	1
6	oyster mushrooms, stems removed, and minced	6
1	large Yukon Gold potato, peeled and chopped	1
1	bunch spinach, washed, stems removed, and cut into thin strips	1
2 cups	fish or chicken stock	500 mL
½ cup	whipping cream (35%)	125 mL
2 cups	1% milk	500 mL
1 pint	pre-shucked oysters with juice, cut into large pieces	500 mL
to taste	salt and freshly ground black pepper	to taste
6 Tbsp	slivered roasted red bell peppers	90 mL
pinch	sweet Hungarian paprika	pinch

METHOD

Heat the butter and oil together in a large saucepan over medium-high heat and sauté the onion for 5 minutes. Add the mushrooms, potatoes, and half of the spinach and cook, stirring, for 5 more minutes. Add the stock and reserved oyster juice. Cover, bring to a boil, and simmer on medium-low heat until the potatoes are soft, about 15 minutes.

Add the cream and simmer for 2 minutes. Purée, using a hand blender, blender, or food processor. When the mixture is very smooth, add the milk and reheat to a simmer. Stir in the coarsely chopped oysters. Cover the pan and cook on medium heat for 2–3 minutes, just until the oysters have plumped and curled around the edges. Stir in the remaining spinach and cook for 30 seconds, until the spinach turns brilliant green.

Season with salt and pepper. Ladle into soup bowls and garnish with red bell pepper and paprika.

Here's something decadent you can whip up to kick off an evening of romance (these briny bivalves have particular powers, you know). Freshly cooked and sliced artichoke hearts are the best choice but canned artichokes are infinitely easier. Serve with a good baguette and a bottle of crisp white wine or champagne. Serves 2 as an entrée, 4 as a starter.

OYSTER & ARTICHOKE STEW

INGREDIENTS

2 cups	fresh, shucked small oysters with juice	500 mL
1	14 oz (398 mL) can artichoke hearts, drained	1
1	lemon, zest of	1
1	medium leek	1
¼ cup	butter	60 mL
2 Tbsp	all-purpose flour	30 mL
1 cup	fish, clam, or chicken broth	250 mL
½ cup	white wine or champagne	125 mL
¼ cup	whipping cream (35%)	60 mL
2 Tbsp	chopped parsley	30 mL
pinch	cayenne pepper	pinch

METHOD

Drain the oysters, reserving ¼ cup (60 mL) of the juice. Set aside. Chop two or three artichokes finely, and quarter the rest. Set aside. Chop the lemon zest finely—you need 1 tsp (5 mL). Set aside.

Discard the tough green top of the leek. Cut the white and pale green part of the leek in half lengthwise and rinse it well under running water. Slice the leek thinly and rinse again. Drain to dry.

In a saucepan, heat the butter over medium heat. Add the leeks and sauté for 5 minutes. Stir in the flour and cook for 2 minutes, then slowly add the broth, stirring constantly until the sauce is smooth and thick.

Stir in the wine and oyster juice and bring to a boil. Add the cream and simmer until the sauce is thickened. Stir in the artichokes, lemon zest, and parsley. Return to a simmer, then add the oysters. In about 3 minutes, when the oysters are just starting to curl around the edges, it's ready. Serve dusted with cayenne pepper.

My friend and Mayne Island neighbor Don McDougall used to serve this at his long-gone, still-missed, now legendary Vancouver restaurant, Mocha Café. I asked him for the important bits for my earlier cookbook, and have fiddled with it—not too much, just added the odd dash or splash—till it comes out like this and seems to delight every oyster fan who ever fell face first into it. Serves 2–4.

MAYNE ISLAND OYSTER STEW

INGREDIENTS

16	fresh, shucked oysters with juice	16
1 cup	dry white wine	250 mL
1 cup	water	250 mL
2–4 slices	smoked bacon (optional), cut into small pieces	2–4
3 Tbsp	vegetable oil for sautéing (optional)	45 mL
3 cups	diced vegetables (such as carrots celery, onions, potatoes, and celeriac)	750 mL
1 cup	whole milk	250 mL
1 cup	whipping cream (35%)	250 mL
2 Tbsp	melted butter	30 mL
to taste	salt and pepper	to taste
pinches	celery salt and paprika	pinches
dash	Worcestershire sauce	dash
to taste	chopped parsley	to taste

METHOD

Poach the oysters in the wine, water, and oyster juice for 4 minutes. Remove the oysters and set aside. Strain and save the stock.

Sauté the bacon, if using, until well cooked. Otherwise, heat enough vegetable oil to cover the bottom of the pan. Add the vegetables and sauté until tender. Add the milk and the poaching liquid to the vegetables and bring to an almost-boil. Skim off any froth and simmer for 10 minutes.

Add the oysters, heavy cream, and butter. Simmer for 3 minutes more.

Season with salt, pepper, celery salt, paprika, and Worcestershire sauce. Toss in the parsley and serve in warm bowls with a baguette or crusty bread.

Panko is crispy Japanese bread crumbs that make a particularly nice coating for fried seafood. Look for it at Asian markets. You can use pre-shucked oysters, sold in jars or plastic containers, for this dish. Serves 6–8.

SAUTÉED OYSTERS IN PANKO CRUST

INGREDIENTS

24	fresh, shucked small oysters	24
2	eggs	2
¼ cup	water	60 mL
2 cups	panko (Japanese bread crumbs)	500 mL
to taste	salt and freshly ground black pepper	to taste
as needed	canola oil, for frying	as needed

METHOD

Preheat the oven to 200°F (95°C).

Pat the oysters dry on paper towels and set aside. Beat together the eggs and water in a small bowl and set aside. Combine the panko with salt and pepper on a plate. Using a fork, dip each oyster in the egg mixture, shaking off any excess liquid, then roll in the seasoned bread crumbs to coat well. Set the coated oysters on a wire rack for 30 minutes.

In a heavy skillet, heat ½ inch (1 cm) of oil to 375°F (190°C) and fry the oysters in batches until golden, about 2 minutes per side. Drain the oysters on a plate lined with paper towels and keep them warm in the preheated oven while you fry the remaining oysters.

Serve the oysters on individual plates, with a dollop of fruit salsa or mayonnaise on the side.

Somewhere in my eating and drinking travels I collected an oyster recipe that's been as much a staple in my kitchen as has Lustau Palo Cortado dry sherry in my bar. It brings together the metallic tang of fresh oysters with herbs and garlic, hot chili, and cold dry sherry. Here's a double batch to pique the palates of the bridge club. Serves 4.

SHERRIED, CHILIED OYSTERS

INGREDIENTS

2 Tbsp	olive oil	30 mL
4	garlic cloves, minced	4
½ cup	tomato paste	125 mL
1½ cups	clam juice or oyster juice, or chicken broth, or combination	375 mL
1 Tbsp	hot chili sauce of choice	15 mL
1	dry chili pepper, for good luck	1
2 Tbsp	ultra-dry sherry (the aforementioned Lustau is ideal)	30 mL
1 tsp	oregano (more if you find it fresh)	5 mL
1 tsp	minced parsley	5 mL
1 quart	fresh, shucked oysters with juice	1 L
to taste	freshly ground black pepper	to taste

METHOD

Heat the oil and sauté the garlic until golden. Stir in the tomato paste, juice or broth, chili sauce, chili pepper, sherry, oregano, and parsley. Blend well and heat through.

Add the oysters. When they commence curling 'round the edges, they're done.

Sprinkle on black pepper and serve at once, with crusty bread, pouring lots more chilled sherry from the extra bottle in the door of the refrigerator, where it's been chilling for the last hour.

Choose a variety of oysters you are partial to. I like Hama Hamas or Olympias from BC, Washington, and Oregon; Malpeques from PEI; and Tatamagouches, Capes, or Blue Points from Atlantic Canada and the north-eastern US. If you like them as Mother Nature made them, try this! Use your very best extra virgin olive oil. Serve champagne. Life is good. Serves 2–4.

OYSTERS AU NATUREL

WITH ROASTED GARLIC & THYME DRIZZLE

INGREDIENTS

12	oysters	12
1 Tbsp	cognac	15 mL
2 Tbsp	berry vinegar	30 mL
⅓ cup	extra virgin olive oil	75 mL
3 Tbsp	mashed roasted garlic	45 mL
1 Tbsp	liquid honey	15 mL
1 tsp	minced fresh thyme	5 mL
1 tsp	minced fresh chives	5 mL
to taste	kosher salt and freshly ground black pepper	to taste
to taste	lemon juice	to taste

METHOD

Shuck the oysters: leave them in the deep lower half of the shell but sever the muscle holding them attached. Combine the remaining ingredients, whisking well to incorporate the garlic. Drizzle over the oysters. Bottoms up.

A dish that's served me well since the afternoon I invented it, which was upon getting stuck in a bottle of Vancouver Island Scrumpy from the Merridale Cider Works. I thought I'd bring it back here for those who (a) love oysters, (b) like real cider, and (c) might have missed it in my last cookbook, over a decade ago. Serves 2.

ANGELS IN E-TYPES (SCRUMPIED OYSTERS)

INGREDIENTS

6	slices Ayrshire bacon	6
6 Tbsp	cold, unsalted butter	90 mL
¼ cup	minced shallots	60 mL
1	serious chili pepper (Scotch bonnet or jalapeño), seeded and minced	1
6 or 12	fresh, shucked oysters with juice (big West Coasters or small Easterners)	6 or 12
½ cup	Merridale Scrumpy or other strong apple cider	125 mL
to taste	salt and pepper	to taste
½ tub	Jersey double cream or ½ cup (125 mL) whipping cream (35%)	90 g
1½ Tbsp	apple cider vinegar	22 mL
2 Tbsp	chopped chives	30 mL

METHOD

Start cooking the bacon in a skillet, hot at first to sear, then medium, until semicrisp. Drain and keep warm. Save a little bacon fat.

Meanwhile, melt half the butter in a sturdy pan. Add the shallots and hot pepper. Stir and cook for 3 minutes on medium heat. Add a little oyster liquid and cook another 2 minutes.

Add the oysters and cook briefly, no more than 2 minutes, until the edges start to curl. Remove the oysters with a slotted spoon and keep warm.

Add 1 Tbsp (15 mL) bacon fat and the scrumpy to the oyster juice. Stir and boil, reducing by half. Add the salt and pepper and cream and cook 1 minute. Swirl in the remaining butter and the apple cider vinegar. Add the oysters and heat through.

Put 1 or 2 oysters on a slice of bacon, roll up à la Angels on Horseback, and secure with toothpicks. Or not. Pour the sauce over and sprinkle the chives on top.

Erin's parents own a beautiful cottage in Washington State where we go for minivacations. Erin always wants oysters, so I like to make a different oyster dish every time. This received 5 stars. Serves 4.

OYSTERS BAKED IN GARLIC & SHERRY FOR ERIN

INGREDIENTS

¾ quart	pre-shucked small oysters	750 mL
1 cup	unsalted butter	250 mL
⅓ cup	sweet sherry	75 mL
4	garlic cloves, minced	4
¼ tsp	sea salt	1 mL
2 tsp	coarsely crushed black pepper	10 mL
6 cups	bread crumbs (use day-old white bread)	1.5 L

METHOD

Preheat the oven to 400°F (200°C). Place the oysters in a single layer in a 9- x 13-inch (23 x 33 cm) baking dish. In a saucepan over low heat, melt the butter. Add the sherry, garlic, salt, and pepper. Add the bread crumbs and toss until well coated. Spread the bread crumbs evenly over the oysters. Do not pack them down. Bake for 20 minutes in the middle of the oven. Turn on the broiler and broil until the top is golden brown, about 3–4 minutes.

Tangy cheese, succulent oysters, and cream-laced leeks make this a delicious and ultrarich appetizer. Makes 12 baked oysters.

BAKED OYSTERS
WITH CREAMY LEEKS & PARMESAN CHEESE

INGREDIENTS

2 Tbsp	olive oil	30 mL
1	medium leek, white and pale green part only, halved lengthwise, washed, and thinly sliced	1
1	garlic clove, chopped	1
1 cup	whipping cream (35%)	250 mL
to taste	salt and freshly ground black pepper	to taste
12	fresh, shucked small or medium oysters left in the half shell	12
¼ cup	freshly grated Parmesan cheese	60 mL

METHOD

Heat the oil in a skillet over medium heat. Add the leek and cook until tender, about 4–5 minutes. Add the garlic and cook 1 minute more. Pour in the cream and cook until it thickens slightly; season with salt and pepper and remove from the heat.

Preheat the oven to 425°F (220°C). Place the shucked oysters on a baking sheet. Divide and spoon the leek mixture over the oysters. Top each oyster with Parmesan cheese. Bake for 10 minutes and serve.

OPTION

To make the oysters sit flat during baking, spread a thick layer of coarse salt on the baking sheet and nestle the shells into the salt until level. If you are hopeless at shucking oysters, try and seek out the pre-shucked oysters on the half shell available in the frozen foods section of some supermarkets and seafood stores. Thaw before using.

PHOTO BY MICHAEL TOURIGNY • FOOD STYLING BY ERIC AKIS

Rich-tasting oysters marry well with equally rich flavors. In this recipe spinach, cream, and Parmesan cheese do the work deliciously. Serves 4.

BAKED OYSTERS
WITH SPINACH & PARMESAN

INGREDIENTS

¼ cup	dry white wine	60 mL
4 cups	packed spinach leaves, stems removed	1 L
1	garlic clove, finely chopped	1
½ cup	whipping cream (35%)	125 mL
to taste	salt and white pepper	to taste
12	fresh, shucked oysters left in the half shell	12
½ cup	freshly grated Parmesan cheese	125 mL

METHOD

Preheat the oven to 450°F (230°C). Bring the wine to a boil in a large, wide skillet over medium-high heat. Add the spinach and cook until it just wilts and the wine and liquid from the spinach evaporate. Add the garlic and whipping cream and cook until the cream thickens slightly. Remove from the heat; season with salt and white pepper.

Place the oysters on a large baking sheet or roasting pan. Top each with a spoonful of the spinach mixture and sprinkle with Parmesan cheese. Bake for 10–12 minutes, until nicely browned and bubbling. Carefully lift the oysters onto 4 appetizer plates. Serve immediately.

I like teaching this dish because the skeptical looks on people's faces change to smiles of bliss very quickly.
Serves 4.

OYSTER PIE

INGREDIENTS

½ lb	fresh washed spinach, stems removed	250 g
2 Tbsp	unsalted butter	30 mL
1 cup	finely diced onion	250 mL
½ cup	finely diced fennel bulb	125 mL
1 cup	dry white wine	250 mL
2 cups	whipping cream (35%)	500 mL
1 tsp	sea salt	5 mL
2 tsp	finely chopped fresh tarragon	10 mL
1 Tbsp	fresh lemon juice	15 mL
2½ lb	russet potatoes, peeled and cut into 1-inch (2.5 cm) chunks	1.25 kg
½ cup	buttermilk, warmed	125 mL
2 Tbsp	unsalted butter at room temperature	30 mL
1 Tbsp	prepared horseradish	15 mL
to taste	sea salt and freshly ground black pepper	to taste

24	fresh, shucked medium oysters	24
½ cup	fine dry bread crumbs	125 mL
to taste	paprika	to taste

METHOD

In a large pot, steam the spinach, using only the water clinging to its leaves. Drain and place on a plate to cool. Squeeze the water out of the spinach and chop coarsely. Set aside.

In a large saucepan melt the butter over medium heat. Add the onion and fennel and sauté until the onion is translucent. Add the white wine, turn the heat to high, and boil until the wine is reduced by half. Add the whipping cream and boil until the mixture is reduced to 1½ cups (375 mL). Stir in the salt, tarragon, and lemon juice. Remove from the heat.

Cover the potatoes with water in a large pot, bring to a boil, and cook until very tender, 15–20 minutes. Drain and return to the pot. Mash the potatoes until smooth. Beat in the buttermilk, then the butter and horseradish. Season with salt and pepper.

Preheat the oven to 425°F (220°C). Place the oysters in an 8-inch (2 L) square baking dish and sprinkle with bread crumbs. Stir the spinach into the cream sauce and pour over the oysters. Spoon the mashed potatoes over the sauce and sprinkle lightly with paprika. Place in the oven and bake for 20–30 minutes, until the mixture is bubbling and the potatoes are lightly browned.

A warming late fall or winter dish, full of great textures and flavors. Serves 4.

CORNMEAL FRIED OYSTERS
WITH RED CABBAGE, SAUSAGE & GARLIC MAYONNAISE

INGREDIENTS

4 cups	thinly sliced red cabbage	1 L
3 Tbsp	apple cider vinegar	45 mL
½ tsp	sea salt	2 mL
1 tsp	sugar	5 mL
⅔ cup	flour	150 mL
⅓ cup	cornmeal	75 mL
½ tsp	sea salt	2 mL
½ tsp	black pepper	2 mL
¼ tsp	turmeric	1 mL
large pinch	cayenne pepper	large pinch
2 Tbsp	vegetable oil	30 mL
2	garlic cloves, minced	2
1 cup	finely diced onion	250 mL
2	hot Italian sausages, skinned	2
½	apple, peeled, cored, and thinly sliced	½
20	fresh, shucked medium oysters, drained	20
	vegetable oil for frying	

METHOD

Combine the red cabbage, vinegar, salt, and sugar. Let it sit while you are preparing the other ingredients.

Mix the flour, cornmeal, salt, pepper, turmeric, and cayenne pepper together. Spread out on a large plate.

Heat the 2 Tbsp (30 mL) oil in a large, heavy skillet over medium heat. Add the garlic and sauté until light gold. Add the onion and sauté until lightly browned. Add the sausages and fry, crumbling with a fork until cooked through. Add the apple and red cabbage and turn the heat to high. Sauté, stirring frequently until the cabbage is glistening and heated through but not soft. Remove from the heat.

Bread the oysters with the cornmeal mixture and place on a plate. Sprinkle the leftover cornmeal mixture over the oysters.

Preheat the oven to 250ºF (120ºC). Heat half an inch (1 cm) of vegetable oil in a large, heavy skillet until a haze forms over the oil. Fry the oysters without over-crowding the pan in several batches until golden brown on both sides. Drain each batch on absorbent paper then transfer to a baking sheet and place in the oven.

When you have finished frying the oysters, reheat the cabbage over high heat, stirring frequently until heated through and tender-crisp. Place on a heated platter and surround with the oysters. Pass the garlic mayonnaise separately.

Garlic Mayonnaise

1	egg yolk	1
1 tsp	Dijon mustard	5 mL
½ cup	vegetable oil	125 mL
½ cup	extra virgin olive oil	125 mL
1	large garlic clove, finely chopped	1
½ tsp	sea salt	2 mL
4 tsp	lemon juice	20 mL

Combine the egg yolk and mustard in the work bowl of a food processor. With the motor running, slowly dribble in the olive and vegetable oil. Mash up the garlic with 1 tsp of sea salt to make a paste. Add it to the food processor along with the lemon juice and pulse a few times to combine. Transfer to a bowl, cover, and refrigerate. May be made up to 2 days in advance.

Ice-cold beer pairs beautifully with these crispy oyster burgers flavored with spicy mayonnaise. Serves 4.

CORNMEAL-CRUSTED OYSTER BURGERS

INGREDIENTS

½ cup	mayonnaise	125 mL
1	lime, juice and zest of	1
3 Tbsp	chopped fresh cilantro	45 mL
½ tsp	cayenne pepper, or to taste	2 mL
½ cup	cornmeal	125 mL
½ cup	bread crumbs	125 mL
pinch	cayenne pepper	pinch
½ tsp	salt	2 mL
½ tsp	black pepper	2 mL
1 cup	all-purpose flour	250 mL
2	large eggs, beaten and mixed with ¼ cup (60 mL) milk	2
12	fresh, shucked medium oysters	12
	vegetable oil	
4	large burger buns, warmed	4
4	lettuce leaves	4
to garnish	sliced tomato and onion	to garnish

METHOD

Combine the mayonnaise, lime juice, lime zest, cilantro, and ½ tsp (2 mL) cayenne pepper in a bowl. Cover and store in the fridge.

Combine the cornmeal, bread crumbs, pinch of cayenne pepper, salt, and black pepper in a wide, shallow dish. Place the flour in another dish, and the egg mixture in a third dish.

Drain the oysters well. Coat them first in flour, shaking off the excess. Dip them in the egg mixture, making sure they are evenly coated. Set in the cornmeal mixture, gently pressing it onto the oysters.

Heat ⅛ inch (3 mm) of vegetable oil in a large skillet over medium-high heat. Fry the oysters for 2 minutes per side, until crispy, golden, and just cooked through. If you are cooking in batches, keep the cooked oysters warm in a 200°F (95°C) oven.

Fill each bun with 3 fried oysters, mayonnaise, and tomato and onion slices. Serve immediately.

Years ago the Wakefield Inn, a pub on BC's Sunshine Coast, invented the ultimate burger. Ironically, it's not grilled. To get the right texture you need to pan-fry the oysters. The Wakefield Inn uses seasoned flour, but I prefer the extra crunch of cornmeal. Serve with a dill pickle, a dollop of potato salad, and a big mug of cold beer. Serves 4.

THE WAKEFIELD INN OYSTER BURGER

INGREDIENTS

1 tsp	ground cumin	5 mL
1 tsp	ground ancho chilies	5 mL
1 tsp	freshly ground black pepper	5 mL
½ cup	cornmeal	125 mL
1 Tbsp	butter	15 mL
1 Tbsp	olive oil	15 mL
12	fresh, shucked medium or large West Coast oysters	12
4	burger buns, toasted and buttered	4
¼ cup	tartar sauce	60 mL
1	bunch green leaf lettuce	1
4	slices crisply cooked bacon	4
1	thinly sliced ripe tomato	1
to taste	salt and pepper	to taste
to garnish	pickle slice and parsley sprigs	to garnish

METHOD

Combine the cumin, ground ancho, pepper, and cornmeal and pour the mixture on a dinner plate. Heat the butter and oil in a heavy skillet over medium-high heat until the butter is sizzling. Lightly coat the oysters in the cornmeal mixture and fry in the oil and butter until crisp on the outside and done inside, about 2–3 minutes per side.

Spread 1 Tbsp (15 mL) of tartar sauce on each toasted and buttered bun. Add a leaf or two of lettuce, 3 of the fried oysters, one crispy slice of bacon (ripped in half), and 1 or 2 slices of tomato. Sprinkle with salt and pepper. Top with the other half bun, and garnish with pickle and a parsley sprig.

CLAMS

They have no face, no place for ears

There's no clam eyes to cry clam tears

—NOFX, "Clams Have Feelings Too

(Actually They Don't)"

ᔈ

EVEN THOUGH I GREW UP IN LANDLOCKED ONTARIO, I WAS NO STRANGER TO CLAMS. Nanny would regularly open a can of baby clams to make her simple version of chowder. She would heat the clams and their juice up with milk, add some pepper, and serve it with a smidge of butter on top and a stack of saltine crackers. The clams were chewy and bland, but the milky broth had a delicious tangy saltiness. Sometimes I would take a clam out of the bowl and study it. What odd creatures these tiny clams were. Nanny was from Nova Scotia and would talk about digging clams as we shared the chowder. I hoped one day to dig clams too.

My wish came true when I was nineteen, on a trip to the East Coast. It was fascinating to watch the clams glide through the sand, trying to avoid the deep probe of the shovel. Some of them didn't get away fast enough and these became my first chowder made from real, live, clams.

I actually like the tangy broth from the clams more than the clams themselves. And because they're usually served hot and steamy, I think of them as winter food.

East and West Coast Clams

The common hard clam (*Mercenaria mercenaria*) is harvested along the East Coast from New Brunswick to Florida. It can be a little confusing because it's sold under different names, depending upon its size and where it's being sold. From small to large, the market names include Little Neck, topneck, Cherrystone, chowder, and Quahog.

The Stimpson or arctic surf clam (*Mactromeris polynyma*) is harvested from the Maritime Provinces and the Gulf of St. Lawrence. Called *hokkigai* in Japanese, the foot of the clam is popular for sushi.

Little Necks are often confused with littlenecks. Little Necks are small, hard-shell clams that get their name from Little Neck Bay in New York. The West Coast littleneck (*Protothaca staminea*) is harvested along with Manila clams. The West Coast littlenecks take longer to open when cooked and have a shorter shelf life.

Manila clams (*Tapes japonica*) were introduced from Asia in the 1930s and are produced in British Columbia and Washington State. Most of British Columbia's production comes from natural beds while in Washington they are primarily farmed. The annual West Coast harvest is about 10 million pounds.

Other clams include the butter clam, razor clam, soft shell, mahogany clam, horse clam, and geoduck. Except for the geoduck, these clams do not have a strong market presence and are usually gathered by individuals.

Storing and Preparing Clams

Clams have been purged of sand for market. They require a bit of cleaning with a stiff brush to remove any sand from their shells. Store them refrigerated and under a damp towel, where they will last from three to four days. Do not soak or leave them in fresh water because this will kill them. Before cooking, check to see that the shells are tightly closed. Gaping shells that don't close when jostled means the clam is dead, and a dead clam is not a tasty clam.

Most people discard clams and mussels that don't open. Italian cookbook author Marcella Hazan states that a clam that does not want to open is one that is trying valiantly to live. After steaming hundreds of pounds of clams, I have to agree with her. Occasionally, a clam will not open. After being manually opened, you may find the shell has no inhabitant or is filled with sand. However, the choice is yours as to how you want to deal with unopened clams.

A bad clam smells bad, and was most likely dead for a while before being cooked. Unfortunately, if you have cooked a bad clam with the other clams, throw all of them away—the smell and flavor will have permeated the whole dish.

What makes this chowder really good is the sweet and tender Manila clams that grow so plentifully in this area. Rather than put bacon in this chowder I like to put a local delicacy called Indian candy. Indian candy is made from sugar-cured salmon bellies that are cut into strips and smoked until they are almost dry. If it is available in your area, add a small handful, finely chopped, when you are sautéing the onions and celery. Serves 6.

CLAM CHOWDER

INGREDIENTS

4 lb	fresh Manila clams, cleaned	1.8 kg
¼ cup	unsalted butter	60 mL
½ cup	diced onions	125 mL
½ cup	diced celery	125 mL
¼ cup	all-purpose flour	60 mL
2 cups	reserved clam nectar, heated	500 mL
to taste	sea salt and freshly ground black pepper	to taste
2 cups	peeled, diced potatoes, cooked until tender and drained	500 mL
1 cup	whipping cream (35%)	250 mL

METHOD

Scrub the clams and place in a large pot. Steam over high heat, shaking the pot occasionally, until clams open. Drain the clams, reserving the juice. Strain the juice. Remove the clams from the shells and chop coarsely.

Melt the butter over low heat in a large heavy pot. Sauté the onion and celery until they are translucent. Add the flour and stir for a few minutes. Slowly whisk in the heated clam nectar, ensuring that there are no lumps. Bring to a boil then reduce to a simmer. Cook for 20 minutes. Season with salt and pepper.

When ready to serve, add the potatoes and heat through. Add the cream and the reserved chopped clams. Bring to a simmer and serve.

Creamy New England–style clam chowder may be classic, but there's something sexier about the Manhattan version—just like its namesake. But if you must have your clam chowder creamy (and don't mind the extra calories), stir in some heavy cream at the end. Divine, dahling! Serves 6–8.

MANHATTAN CLAM CHOWDER

INGREDIENTS

2	thick slices smoky bacon, finely chopped	2
1	large onion, finely chopped	1
2	celery stalks, finely chopped	2
1 Tbsp	all-purpose flour	15 mL
3 cups	water or chicken broth	750 mL
1	14 oz (398 mL) can tomatoes, chopped	1
1	large carrot, grated or finely chopped	1
2 cups	peeled and cubed potatoes	500 mL
1 tsp	dried thyme	5 mL
2	bay leaves	2
pinch	cayenne pepper	pinch
2	14 oz (398 mL) cans baby clams, including juice	2
½–1 cup	whipping cream (35%) (optional)	125–250 mL
to taste	salt and freshly ground black pepper	to taste

METHOD

In a large soup pot over medium-high heat, fry the bacon until it begins to crisp. Add the onion and celery, and cook for 5 minutes or until the vegetables soften and start to brown. Stir in the flour. Slowly stir in the water, then add the tomatoes, carrots, potatoes, thyme, bay leaves, and cayenne. Bring to a boil, cover, and reduce the heat to low. Simmer for 20 minutes.

Discard the bay leaves. Stir in the clams and their juice and heat to a boil. Reduce the heat to low and stir in the cream, if using. Simmer for 10 more minutes. Season to taste with salt and pepper before serving.

Canned clams are inexpensive and easy to use—two good reasons to make this hearty, "stick to your ribs" chowder. Serves 4.

THICK & CREAMY CLAM CHOWDER

INGREDIENTS

1	10 oz (284 mL) can clams	1
3	slices bacon, finely chopped	3
1	small onion, finely chopped	1
2	celery ribs, finely chopped	2
3 Tbsp	all-purpose flour	45 mL
1	10 oz (284 mL) can clam nectar	1
1	13 oz (375 mL) can 2% evaporated milk	1
2	medium potatoes, peeled and cubed	2
pinch	dried thyme	pinch
1	bay leaf	1
to taste	salt and white pepper	to taste

METHOD

Drain the clams, reserve the liquid, and set both aside. Cook the bacon in a soup pot until slightly crispy. Add the onion and celery and cook, stirring, for 3–4 minutes. Mix in the flour until well combined. Slowly stir in the reserved clam juice, clam nectar, and evaporated milk. Add the potatoes, thyme, and bay leaf. Simmer for 10 minutes. Add the reserved clams, season with salt and pepper, and simmer for 10 minutes more, or until the potatoes are tender.

TIP

Clam nectar is often sold in cans. In some areas it is called clam juice.

OPTION

For added color, add ¼ cup (60 mL) of finely diced carrot and ¼ cup (60 mL) of finely diced red pepper to the chowder with the onion and celery. If you prefer, use other herbs, such as dill or tarragon, instead of thyme.

The secret to the amazing flavor of this soup is the long, slow cooking of the onions—do not rush or scrimp on the time needed to cook them. Serves 4–6.

CHORIZO & CLAM SOUP

INGREDIENTS

¼ cup	butter	60 mL
¼ cup	olive oil	60 mL
3	large onions, diced	3
6	garlic cloves, chopped	6
4	chorizo sausages	4
1	bunch parsley, minced	1
4 cups	veal or chicken stock	1 L
4 cups	fish stock	1 L
1	13 oz (375 mL) can whole clams	1
4 lb	fresh clams, cleaned	1.8 kg

METHOD

Melt the butter with the olive oil in a large heavy-bottomed pot over medium heat. Add the onion and garlic and sauté until soft, about 10 minutes. Remove the chorizo casings and crumble the sausage into the onion. Stir in the parsley, cover the pan, reduce the heat, and slowly simmer for 30–45 minutes with the lid on the pot.

Add the veal and fish stocks, bring to a boil, and simmer for at least 10 minutes. Add the canned clams along with the juice in the can, and the live clams. Cover and cook until the clams open. Discard any unopened clams. Serve immediately.

I love this heady combination of flavors with the smoothness of the cream. Add some boiled, sliced potatoes to the cooking pot for an exotic chowder. Serves 4.

CLAMS WITH BACON, OLIVES & TOMATOES

INGREDIENTS

½ lb	sliced bacon, cut into ½-inch (1 cm) pieces	250 g
4	garlic cloves, minced	4
¼ cup	finely chopped shallots	60 mL
½ cup	dry white wine	125 mL
½ cup	drained, canned plum tomatoes, finely chopped	125 mL
12	large, good-quality green olives, pitted and chopped	12
½ cup	whipping cream (35%) or crème fraîche	125 mL
3 lb	fresh Manila clams, cleaned	1.5 kg
2 Tbsp	finely chopped fresh parsley	30 mL

METHOD

In a large pot, cook the bacon on low heat until crisp. Remove and reserve the bacon and discard all the fat except 1 Tbsp (15 mL). Turn the heat to high and add the garlic and shallots to the pot. When they sizzle, add the wine, tomatoes, olives, whipping cream or crème fraîche, and clams.

Cover tightly until the clams open, shaking the pot occasionally. When the clams have opened, add the bacon and parsley and shake to mix. Serve in heated bowls.

This is also very good with mussels and can be served with steamed rice for a main course. It's quickly assembled and cooked—bonus! Serves 4.

CLAMS STEAMED IN SPICY COCONUT LIME BROTH

INGREDIENTS

1	14 oz (398 mL) can unsweetened coconut milk	1
½ cup	canned or bottled clam nectar	125 mL
1 cup	canned plum tomatoes, well drained and finely diced	250 mL
1 Tbsp	fresh cilantro leaves	15 mL
¼ tsp	turmeric	1 mL
1	jalapeño pepper, finely chopped	1
2 Tbsp	freshly squeezed lime juice	30 mL
1	lime, thinly sliced	1
3 lb	fresh Manila clams, cleaned	1.5 kg

METHOD

In a large pot combine all the ingredients except the clams. Bring to a boil and add the clams. Cover and cook until the clams open, shaking the pot occasionally. Ladle the clams and broth into heated bowls and serve.

Another true tapas combination—you'll find this little nosh in Spanish bars in cities like Barcelona in the north and Malaga in the south. Serves 2–4.

GARLIC CLAMS

INGREDIENTS

¼ cup	extra virgin olive oil	60 mL
½ cup	minced onion	125 mL
4	garlic cloves, minced	4
½ cup	dry white wine	125 mL
1	dried chili pepper, whole	1
3–4 lb	fresh small clams, cleaned	1.5–1.8 kg
2 Tbsp	finely chopped Italian parsley	30 mL
4	lemon wedges	4

METHOD

In a large saucepan or wok, heat the oil over medium heat. Cook the onion and garlic for 5 minutes, until soft and fragrant. Add the wine and chili pepper and bring to a boil. Simmer until the wine is reduced by half.

Add the clams to the pan and increase the heat to high. Cover the pan and steam until the clams are open, about 5 minutes. Remove from the heat.

Transfer the steamed clams to a large serving dish and discard the chili pepper. Sprinkle with parsley and serve with lemon wedges to squeeze overtop.

The vermouth and curry really bring out the flavor of the clams. Don't forget the best part: dipping your bread in the sauce. Serves 4.

CLAMS IN DRY VERMOUTH & CURRY BROTH

INGREDIENTS

3 lb	clams	1.5 kg
1	onion, diced	1
1 cup	dry white vermouth (Noilly Prat preferred)	250 mL
pinch	curry powder	pinch
½ cup	whipping cream (35%)	125 mL
pinch	pepper	pinch
2 Tbsp	finely chopped parsley, plus more for garnish	30 mL

METHOD

Clean and wash the clams. Combine all the remaining ingredients in a heavy-bottomed pan and then add the clams. Cover the pan and bring to a boil. Cook the clams for about 7 minutes until they all open. Serve in a deep bowl and garnish with chopped parsley.

I prefer my Spaghetti alle Vongole (Spaghetti with Clam Sauce) without tomatoes, but many classic preparations include them. If you want to use tomatoes, add 1 lb (500 g) to the oil and garlic and allow to reduce for 1 hour. Whether or not you add tomatoes, the key is the reduction of the sauce. The addition of good, fresh Italian parsley is a must at the end. Serves 6.

SPAGHETTI ALLE VONGOLE

INGREDIENTS

4 lb	clams in the shell	1.8 kg
	or	
1	18 oz (504 mL) can baby clams in water, drained and liquid reserved	1
½ cup	extra virgin olive oil	125 mL
6	garlic cloves, chopped	6
1 tsp	crushed red chili flakes	5 mL
1 lb	dried spaghetti (preferably Barilla)	500 g
1 cup	white wine	250 mL
2	12 oz (375 mL) bottles clam nectar	2
to taste	kosher salt and freshly ground black pepper	to taste
¼ cup	chopped fresh Italian parsley	60 mL

METHOD

Thoroughly scrub the clams and rinse them well. Place them in a large skillet over moderate heat, covered, until all the shells have opened, about 2–3 minutes. Discard any unopened clams. Lift the clams from the pan with a slotted spoon, set them aside, and cover with foil or a lid to keep warm.

Pour the oil into a large skillet over medium heat and add the garlic. Sauté for a minute or so, but do not brown. Add the chili flakes and stir well. At the same time, bring a large saucepan of salted water to a boil, add the spaghetti, and cook until al dente.

Add the white wine, clam nectar, and any remaining clam liquid (cooking liquid and/or canned clam liquid) to the garlic and chili flakes. Stir over high heat until it is a thick consistency, about 10 minutes. A nice, thick film of oil should form over the sauce. Drain the spaghetti and toss with the sauce. Season with salt and pepper, scatter the clams on top, sprinkle with parsley, and serve.

The sweetness of the corn and saltiness of the clams sing out in harmony. Serves 2 as a main course, 4 as an appetizer.

LINGUINE

WITH MANILA CLAMS & CORN

INGREDIENTS

1½ lb	Manila clams, scrubbed	750 g
2 Tbsp	water	30 mL
⅓ cup	olive oil	75 mL
2	garlic cloves, peeled and thinly sliced	2
½ cup	white wine	125 mL
1 Tbsp	finely chopped parsley	15 mL
⅛ tsp	chili flakes, or to taste	0.5 mL
½ lb	dried linguine	250 g
1	ear of corn, kernels cut off (and cob reserved), about ½ cup (125 mL)	1
¼ cup	freshly grated Parmesan cheese	60 mL

METHOD

Place the clams and water in a pot with a tight-fitting lid. Cook over high heat until the clams open. Remove the clams from their shells and swish them around in the clam liquor to remove any sand. Chop the clams coarsely. Strain the liquor through a coffee filter or paper towels to remove any sand and reserve.

Heat the olive oil over medium heat and sauté the sliced garlic until golden. Add the white wine and cook until reduced by half. Add the clam liquor and reduce by half again. Remove from the heat and stir in the clams, parsley, and chili flakes.

Bring a large pot of salted water to boil and add the linguine. When the water returns to a boil add the corn cob and corn kernels. Cook until the pasta is tender but firm to the bite. Drain and return the pasta to the pot, discarding the corn cob. Quickly reheat the sauce and toss with the pasta. Add the Parmesan cheese and toss a few more times. Serve immediately in heated bowls.

This classic pasta dish is so simple and delicious you'll be making it at least once a month. Remember that your final dish is only as good as the ingredients you use, so don't skimp on the quality of the white wine. Rule of thumb: if it ain't good enough to drink, it ain't good enough to cook with. Serves 6.

LINGUINE WITH CLAMS, CHORIZO & WHITE WINE

INGREDIENTS

2 lb	live clams	1 kg
3 lb	chorizo sausage	1.5 kg
6 Tbsp	olive oil	90 mL
4	garlic cloves	4
1 Tbsp	smoked paprika	15 mL
6	large tomatoes, diced	6
3 cups	good white wine	750 mL
1½ lb	fresh linguine	750 g
to taste	salt and pepper	to taste

METHOD

Clean the clams, removing any mud or visible dirt. Heat a pan to medium-high heat with half the olive oil. Meanwhile, remove the casing from the chorizo sausages and chop them into bite-sized slices. Crush the garlic and add the sausage and garlic to the pan to sauté. Take care not to burn the garlic.

After a couple of minutes, add the smoked paprika, diced tomatoes, white wine, and clams. Cover the saucepan and leave to steam for 6–10 minutes or until the clams open and the sauce has thickened slightly. Stir occasionally.

Drop the pasta into a large saucepan of boiling, salted water. Return to the boil and cook for 1 minute. Drain, toss with olive oil, and divide between four plates. Ladle the clam, chorizo, and white wine sauce over the top and serve immediately.

This pizza illustrates that the simplest ingredients, thoughtfully combined, can create the best possible things to eat. For the best impression, eat it while watching the sun set. *Makes one 16-inch (40 cm) pizza.*

FRESH MANILA CLAM PIZZA

INGREDIENTS

1	recipe Basic Pizza Dough (see recipe next page)	1
2 lb	Manila clams, scrubbed	1 kg
¼ cup	water	60 mL
¼ cup	olive oil	60 mL
2	garlic cloves, minced	2
¼ cup	white wine	60 mL
2 Tbsp	finely chopped parsley	30 mL
⅛ tsp	chili flakes	0.5 mL
¼ cup	freshly grated Parmesan cheese	60 mL

METHOD

Prepare the pizza dough (see recipe next page). While the pizza dough is rising, place the clams and water in a pot with a tight-fitting lid. Cook over high heat until the clams open. Remove from the heat. When the clams are cool enough to handle, remove them from their shells and swish them around in the clam liquor to remove any sand. Chop the clams coarsely. Strain the liquor through a coffee filter or paper towels to remove any sand. Reserve the clams and liquor.

Heat the olive oil over medium heat and sauté the garlic until golden. Add the white wine and cook until it is reduced by half. Add the clam liquor and cook until reduced by half. Remove from the heat and add the parsley and chili flakes.

Preheat the oven to 400°F (200°C). Press the pizza dough into an oiled 16-inch (40 cm) pizza pan, making deep indentations with your fingers. Place in the oven

Method continues on the next page . . .

and bake for 10 minutes, until the dough will slide easily off the pan. Spread the clam liquor mixture evenly over the dough. Slide directly onto the oven rack and bake for about 15 minutes, until the bottom of the pizza is lightly browned.

Spread the clams and Parmesan cheese over the crust and bake for 5 more minutes. Remove from the oven and let rest for 5 minutes before cutting.

Basic Pizza Dough
Makes one 16-inch (40 cm) pizza crust.

1½ cups	lukewarm water	375 mL
1 tsp	granulated sugar	5 mL
1 Tbsp	yeast	15 mL
¼ cup	olive oil	60 mL
½ tsp	sea salt	2 mL
2½–3 cups	unbleached white flour, plus more for kneading	625–750 mL

Basic Pizza Dough

Combine the water and sugar in a large bowl. Sprinkle the yeast over the surface and let work for 10 minutes.

Stir in the olive oil and salt. Beat in the flour 1 cup (250 mL) at a time until the dough is too hard to beat. Sprinkle about 1 cup (250 mL) of flour onto a flat surface. Scrape the dough out of the bowl and knead it, adding flour as necessary until the dough is smooth and resilient to the touch, about 10 minutes. Place the dough in a large bowl and pour a bit of olive oil over it. Roll the dough around the bowl to coat it thoroughly with the oil. Cover loosely with plastic wrap or a clean cloth and let rise in a warm place until doubled in bulk, about 2 hours.

Punch down the dough. Lightly oil a 16-inch (40 cm) pizza pan. Roll out and press the dough onto the pan.

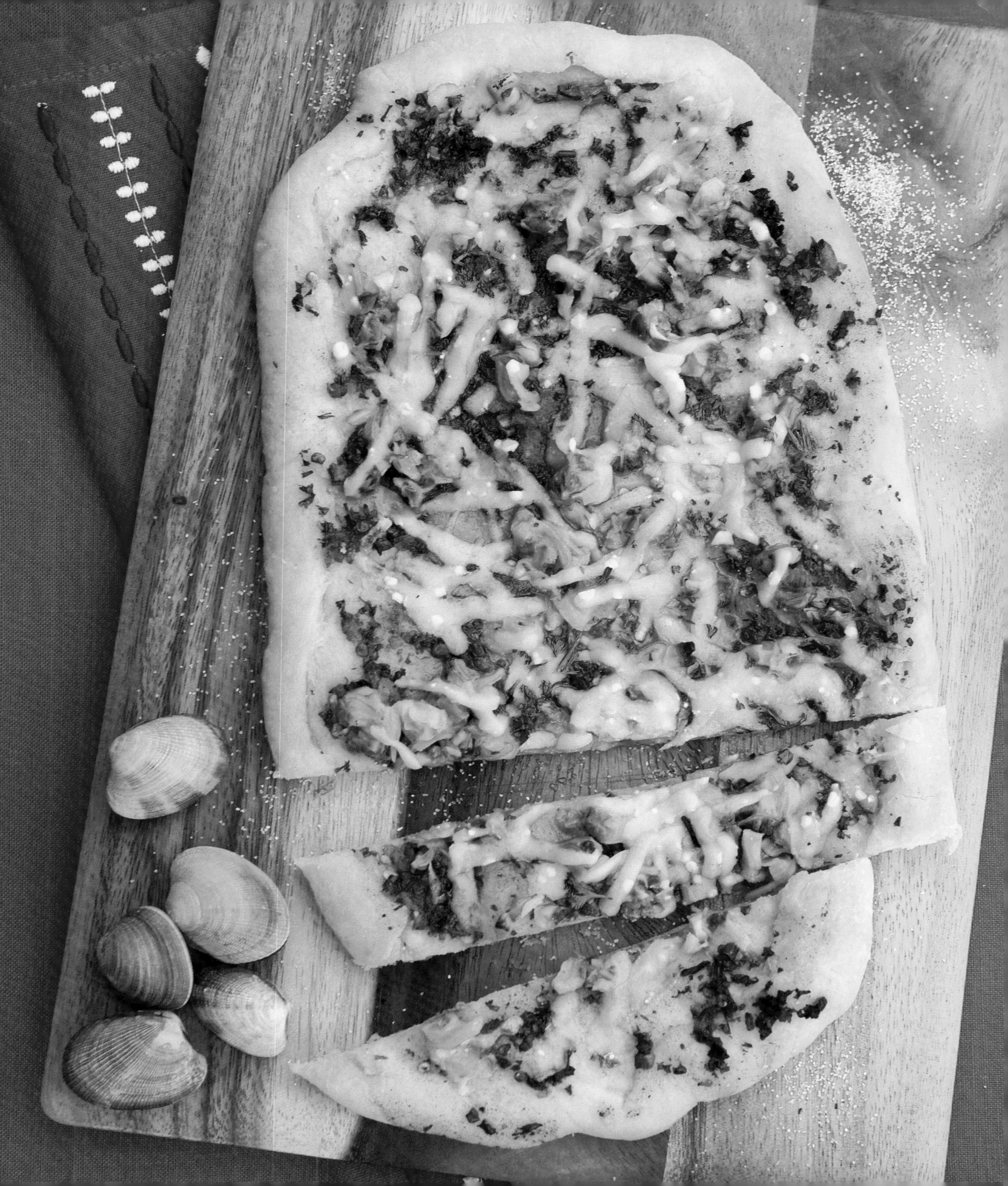

PHOTO BY TRACY KUSIEWICZ • FOOD STYLING BY IRENE MCGUINESS

The foil locks in the steam and cooking juices, making this a quick and tasty way to cook clams. Serves 2.

FOIL-BARBECUED CLAMS

INGREDIENTS

2 lb	fresh clams	1 kg
¼ cup	dry white wine	60 mL
2 Tbsp	melted butter	30 mL
2	garlic cloves, crushed	2
1 Tbsp	chopped fresh parsley	15 mL
to taste	freshly ground black pepper	to taste
½	lemon, juice of	½

METHOD

Preheat the barbecue to medium-high. Cut 2 sheets of foil, each 24 x 12 inches (60 x 30 cm), and place one on top of the other. Place the clams in the center of the foil. Pull up the edges of the foil so that when you add the liquid it won't run out.

Combine the wine, butter, garlic, parsley, pepper, and lemon juice in a bowl. Spoon the mixture over the clams. Seal the clams inside the foil. Grill for 5 minutes, or until the clams just open. Peek inside the foil to see how they are doing, but be careful of the hot steam. Empty into serving bowls and enjoy.

OPTION

Use an equal amount of mussels instead of clams. If you have a ripe medium tomato, chop it finely and add it to the wine mixture. For a more intense herb taste, replace mild-tasting parsley with basil or oregano. For a more filling meal, serve the clams on a bed of fettuccine.

MUSSELS

So, have you heard about the oyster

who went to a disco and

pulled a mussel?

—Billy Connolly

᷾

I ONCE COLLECTED MUSSELS OFF THE ROCKS IN TOFINO AND COOKED THEM. The flavor of the broth was incredible but the mussels were sandy enough to be inedible. Call me foolish, but I don't regret the experience.

Like their fellow bivalve the oyster, mussels can be either uptown or downtown in style. Although they are known as the "poor man's shellfish," they turn up in suave preparations— served as fricassees, paired with saffron, white wine, and cream, and chilled in tangy vinaigrettes.

Mussels with french fries and a real, garlicky aioli is definitely downtown. The height of uptown is the mussel mousse at Roger Vergé's Le Moulin de Mougins in France, a mousse that was as light as a cloud. Although mussel mousse may not sound very appealing, in the hands of a master it was sublime.

East and West Coast Mussels

Around 80 percent of the mussels we eat in North America come from the East Coast, where almost 40 million pounds are cultivated every year. Like all bivalves, they're best when not spawning. During the warmer months, their meat is wizened and they are quick to perish.

Shellfish farmers Dale Williamson and Martin Ellis, in British Columbia, really respect mussels. They cultivate them off Quadra Island and won't sell them during spawning season. They came up with the idea of breeding the native Pacific blue mussel while tending their oyster beds. Mussels grew on everything including

Dale's and Martin's oysters. Noting their sweetness and the fact that one in a thousand sported golden flesh, they began to breed those with the most desirable characteristics. These honey mussels are amazing—the best I've ever eaten.

Mussels are cultured by three basic methods. The most popular is rope culture with the mussels in mesh stockings that are suspended from ropes in the water. These ropes are anchored at the bottom and suspended using a brightly colored lobster buoy for a float. The *bouchot* method is common in Europe (which uses posts instead of ropes) as is the beach or bottom culture.

Mussels anchor themselves to surfaces with tough, brown fibers called the byssal threads (or simply "byssus"), which are commonly known as the "beard."

When mussels are steamed, you'll notice that some are orange, and some are ivory colored. The orange mussels are mature females, and the ivory ones are males and immature females.

Storing and Preparing Mussels

Store mussels in wide, uncovered containers that allow for drainage and ventilation. You can use a thick, folded towel in the bottom of a container. Never store mussels in direct contact with melted ice or water.

Just before cooking, inspect your mussels. Mussels that don't close when tapped or jostled should be discarded before cooking. Check them over for mud on the shells. Rinse these thoroughly, and give all the other live ones a brief rinse in cold water.

Remove the beard just before cooking by grasping it firmly and pulling it down towards the smaller end of the shell. Occasionally, you will find a small pea crab inside a mussel (or other bivalve). They are not harmful to humans and I find them quite fascinating to look at. Although it was once thought that pea crabs did no harm to their hosts, it has been found that their activities do cause some damage to the delicate gills of bivalves. Because of this, pea crabs are now considered parasites.

A mussel that won't open is not necessarily bad; it may be trying valiantly to live. After observing perhaps a ton of mussels being cooked, I've never found that a noncompliant mussel was bad; the bad mussels should have been weeded out when you initially sorted through them. Occasionally I'll find a mussel that won't open and it will be empty inside. However, the choice is yours as to how you want to deal with unopened mussels.

One of the best tips for eating mussels comes from Julia Child. Use an empty pair of shells like a pair of tongs and use it to pluck the waiting-to-be-eaten mussels from their shells. And most mussel lovers know that scooping up the broth and sipping from the shell is the best way to savor it.

Make this, and you'll understand why these typically French flavors for mussels are classic. Serves 4.

MUSSEL SOUP
WITH SAFFRON & THYME

INGREDIENTS

1	bunch fresh thyme	1
3	egg yolks	3
¾ cup	whipping cream (35%)	175 mL
6 Tbsp	unsalted butter	90 mL
1	large onion, thinly sliced	1
2 lb	fresh mussels, cleaned	1 kg
1 cup	dry white wine	250 mL
1	leek, julienned	1
1	carrot, julienned	1
1	celery stalk, julienned	1
pinch	saffron	pinch
to taste	salt and freshly ground black pepper	to taste

METHOD

Wash the thyme and remove the leaves from the stalks. Reserve the thyme stems and chop the leaves. Whisk the egg yolks and cream together. Set aside. Heat 5 Tbsp (75 mL) of the butter in a large pot with a tight-fitting lid. Add the onions and thyme stalks. Sauté gently for a few moments, and then add the mussels and wine. Cover and cook over high heat. Shake the pan after a few minutes. When all the mussels have opened, drain them and reserve the broth. Remove the mussels from the shells. Strain the broth through a cheesecloth, put in a clean saucepan, and bring to a boil.

In another pan, gently sweat the leeks, carrots, and celery with the saffron in the remaining butter for a few moments. Add 1 Tbsp (15 mL) of chopped thyme leaves and then pour in the boiling stock. Add the mussels and the cream and egg yolk mixture.

Whisking all the time, bring back to a simmer and remove from the heat immediately. Season and serve.

Saffron gives this bisque its deep rusty red color. What's the difference between a bisque and a soup? About 2 bucks a bowl! Har har. Actually, a bisque tends to be seafood-based and thicker than a regular soup. There's a complex rich flavor in this soup that's achieved by poaching the mussels in white wine. Be sure to have lots of very hot baguette and very cold butter to go along with this one. Serves 6.

SAFFRON MUSSEL BISQUE

INGREDIENTS

1 cup	water	250 mL
1½ cups	white wine	375 mL
2 lb	fresh mussels, cleaned	1 kg
3 Tbsp	butter	45 mL
1 Tbsp	olive oil	15 mL
1	onion, diced	1
2	garlic cloves, crushed	2
1	leek (bulb only), diced	1
½ tsp	crushed fenugreek seeds	2 mL
1½ Tbsp	all-purpose flour	22 mL
12	saffron threads, steeped in 1 Tbsp (15 mL) of boiling water	12
1¼ cups	chicken broth	310 mL
2 Tbsp	whipping cream (35%)	30 mL
to taste	salt and pepper	to taste
pinch	cayenne	pinch
1 Tbsp	chopped fresh parsley	15 mL

METHOD

In a saucepan, bring the water and wine to a boil. Add the mussels. Cover and cook over high heat, shaking the pan frequently, until the shells are open (about 4–5 minutes). Strain the mussels, reserving the liquid. Discard any mussels that remain closed.

In a large saucepan, heat the butter and oil over medium-high heat. Add the onion, garlic, leek, and fenugreek seeds and cook for 5 minutes. Stir in the flour and continue cooking for 1 minute. Add the saffron water, 2½ cups (625 mL) of the reserved mussel cooking liquid, and the chicken broth. Bring to a boil, cover, and simmer for about 15 minutes.

Meanwhile, remove all but 12 of the mussels from their shells. Add all the mussels to the soup and heat through (2 minutes). Add the whipping cream and combine. Season with salt, pepper, cayenne, and parsley. Ladle the soup into bowls and garnish with parsley sprigs. Add two mussels in the shell to each bowl.

Tomato, garlic, and basil give this eye-appealing soup Italian-style flair. It makes a great starter, but you can also make a meal out of it by serving it with warm slices of olive bread or focaccia. Serves 4.

TOMATO SOUP
WITH MUSSELS & FRESH BASIL

INGREDIENTS

1 Tbsp	olive oil	15 mL
2	garlic cloves, chopped	2
½ cup	dry white wine	125 mL
1 lb	fresh mussels, cleaned	500 g
1	28 oz (796 mL) can crushed tomatoes	1
pinch	sugar	pinch
2 cups	fish, chicken, or vegetable stock	500 mL
2 Tbsp	finely chopped fresh basil	30 mL
2 Tbsp	finely chopped fresh parsley	30 mL
¼ cup	freshly grated Parmesan cheese	60 mL
to taste	salt and freshly cracked black pepper	to taste

METHOD

Heat the oil in a pot over medium-high heat. Add the garlic and cook for 1 minute.

Add the wine and bring to a boil. Add the mussels, cover, and cook until they just open. Using a slotted spoon, transfer the mussels to a platter and set aside to cool to room temperature. Add the tomatoes, sugar, and stock to the soup pot. Adjust the heat to a gentle simmer and cook for 10 minutes. Meanwhile, remove the top shell from each mussel and discard. Arrange the meat-filled halves in 4 soup bowls. When the soup has simmered for 10 minutes, stir in half the basil, parsley, and cheese. Season with salt and pepper. Spoon the soup over the mussels. Sprinkle with the remaining basil, parsley, and cheese, and serve.

OPTION

Make this soup with fresh clams instead of mussels. The procedure is the same; simply replace one mollusk for the other.

For a richer flavor, whisk 4 egg yolks with 2 Tbsp (30 mL) 35% cream and stir into the soup. Cook slowly, stirring constantly until thickened slightly, and serve at once. For a lighter soup, blend half the mussels with 1 cup (250 mL) of the soup until smooth. Return the mixture to the soup. This optional liaison brings this soup to a higher level of elegance. Serves 6.

MUSSEL MOUCLADE

INGREDIENTS

6 Tbsp	unsalted butter	90 mL
1	medium onion, finely chopped	1
3	garlic cloves, finely chopped	3
3 lb	fresh mussels, cleaned	1.5 kg
1 cup	white wine	250 mL
1	leek, cut in half, washed and drained	1
1	medium carrot, peeled and chopped	1
½ tsp	curry powder	2 mL
pinch	saffron	pinch
1 Tbsp	flour	15 mL
2 cups	cold water	500 mL
2 cups	chicken stock	500 mL
1 cup	whipping cream (35%)	250 mL
to taste	salt and freshly ground black pepper	to taste
½	bunch fresh parsley, washed and chopped	½

METHOD

In a large pot, melt half the butter over medium-low heat. Add the onion and garlic and cover, until soft and translucent. Add the mussels and white wine. Cover and turn the heat to high, shaking the pot every minute to mix the ingredients. Cook just until all the mussels have opened. Drain the mussels, reserving the liquid.

In the same pot over medium-low heat, melt the remaining butter. Add the leek and carrot; cook for a few minutes. Add the curry powder, saffron, and flour and cook for another few minutes, stirring.

Gradually add the cold water, chicken stock, and reserved mussel liquid. Bring to a boil, season with salt and pepper and simmer, uncovered, for 15 minutes.

Remove the mussel meat from the shells and chop finely. Reduce the heat to low; add the chopped mussels to the soup with the cream and parsley. Cover and simmer (without boiling) to infuse the flavors and heat the soup through. Adjust the seasoning and serve hot.

A big bowl of mussels steamed in white wine can be ready to eat in 5 minutes, if you've got them prepped and ready. Use a crisp Sancerre or New Zealand Sauvignon Blanc in the recipe, and chill another one for sipping. Works as a main dish or as an appetizer for a French bistro meal—pass the *pommes frites* with mayonnaise and fill a bowl with fresh figs for dessert. Serves 2 as a main course with bread or 4 as an appetizer.

MOULES MARINIÈRES

INGREDIENTS

3	Roma tomatoes	3
2 Tbsp	butter	30 mL
1 Tbsp	extra virgin olive oil	15 mL
2	shallots, minced	2
2	garlic cloves, minced	2
3	green onions, chopped	3
1 cup	white wine	250 mL
2 lb	large fresh mussels, cleaned	1 kg
to taste	salt and freshly ground black pepper	to taste
2 Tbsp	Italian parsley, chopped	30 mL

METHOD

Seed the tomatoes by cutting them in half across the middle and squeezing them gently to remove the seeds. Chop the tomatoes into small cubes.

In a large pot or wok, heat the butter and olive oil over medium-high heat. Sauté the shallots and garlic for 5 minutes until soft. Add the green onion and tomato to the pan and sauté for 2 minutes. Add the wine and bring to a boil, then cook together for 2 minutes.

Add the mussels and cover the pan. Steam for 5 minutes, shaking the pan, until the mussels have opened. Discard any that don't open.

Season with salt and pepper and stir in the parsley. Divide the mussels and cooking liquid between 2 or 4 deep soup bowls.

I like to use Salt Spring Island mussels because they are tastier than East Coast mussels, and they are local. Serves 4.

SALT-ROASTED MUSSELS

WITH MALT VINEGAR AIOLI

INGREDIENTS

3 lb	fresh mussels, cleaned	1.5 kg
½ cup	rock salt	125 mL
¼ cup	malt vinegar	60 mL
1 tsp	lemon juice	5 mL
3	egg yolks	3
½ tsp	minced garlic	2 mL
½ tsp	salt	2 mL
½ tsp	black pepper	2 mL
1 cup	extra virgin olive oil	250 mL

METHOD

Preheat the oven to 500°F (260°C).

Drain any excess water from the mussels. Place them close together in a single layer in an ovenproof dish. Sprinkle the salt over the mussels. Bake for 5 minutes, until the mussels are open. In a mixing bowl, combine the vinegar, lemon juice, egg yolks, garlic, salt, and pepper. Slowly add the olive oil, whisking until it has become a thick, mayonnaise-like sauce.

Divide the mussels among 4 bowls. Serve the aioli over the mussels or serve it separately as a dipping sauce.

This is easy and delicious. You can prepare this dish up to 8 hours in advance—to the point before the mussels are broiled—and refrigerate. When ready to serve, just pop them under the broiler. Serves 8 as an appetizer, 4 as a main course.

MOULES BRÛLÉES

INGREDIENTS

1½ lb	fresh mussels, cleaned	750 g
¼ cup	dry white wine	60 mL
1 cup	mayonnaise	250 mL
2 tsp	minced garlic	10 mL
1 Tbsp	minced parsley	15 mL
1 Tbsp	minced chives	15 mL
1	lemon, grated rind of	1
1 Tbsp	lemon juice	15 mL

METHOD

In a large covered pot, steam the mussels with the white wine over high heat until they open. Strain the mussels and reserve the liquid, passing it through a cheesecloth to remove any sand. Return the liquid to a boil and reduce to about 2 Tbsp (30 mL). Let cool.

Remove the top shells of the mussels and discard. Place the bottom half with the mussels on a baking sheet. Mix the remaining ingredients together including the mussel liquid and spoon over the mussels. Preheat the broiler and broil the mussels about 6 inches (15 cm) from the heat until lightly browned.

The Bloody Caesar is one of those drinks that's bloody perfect for any bloody occasion. This seafood creation is inspired by the classic Canadian drink and even we have to admit, it's bloody genius. Serves 2 as an appetizer.

BLOODY CAESAR–STEAMED MUSSELS

INGREDIENTS

2 Tbsp	extra virgin olive oil	30 mL
1	small onion, finely chopped	1
2	garlic cloves, minced	2
1 cup	Clamato juice	250 mL
¼ cup	vodka	60 mL
2	plum tomatoes, chopped	2
2 Tbsp	chopped celery leaves	30 mL
1 Tbsp	fresh lemon juice	15 mL
2 tsp	horseradish sauce	10 mL
1 tsp	Worcestershire sauce	5 mL
½ tsp	celery salt	2 mL
dash	Tabasco sauce	dash
to taste	freshly ground black pepper	to taste
1 lb	fresh mussels, cleaned	500 g

METHOD

Heat the oil in a large stockpot over medium heat. Add the onion and garlic and cook for 2–3 minutes until softened. Add the Clamato juice, vodka, tomatoes, celery leaves, lemon juice, horseradish, Worcestershire sauce, celery salt, Tabasco sauce, and black pepper and stir. Add the mussels, cover, and steam over high heat until the mussels open, about 4–5 minutes.

Transfer to a bowl and serve with warm and crusty bread or spoon over cooked linguine for a complete meal.

Wine and cream are the most common simmering agents for mussels, but beer adds a great flavor, and goes so well with mustard seed that we often prefer it to the classics. A dark beer such as a stout or porter adds an intense sweet flavor and aroma, whereas a wheat or Oktoberfest beer adds a light and grainy taste. Be sure to have a loaf of rye or whole wheat bread handy for dipping into the sauce. Serves 6 generously.

MUSSELS IN BEER

WITH MUSTARD SEED, ONION & HERBS

INGREDIENTS

2 Tbsp	olive oil	30 mL
1	onion, thinly sliced	1
2	garlic cloves, sliced	2
6 lb	fresh mussels, cleaned	2.7 kg
3 cups	beer	750 mL
1	lemon, sliced	1
1½ Tbsp	dry mustard seed	22 mL
2	fresh thyme sprigs	2
2	fresh tarragon sprigs	2
2	fresh mint sprigs	2
2	fresh marjoram sprigs	2
1½ tsp	salt	7 mL
to taste	pepper	to taste

METHOD

In a large stockpot, heat the oil over medium-high heat. Add the onion and sauté for 5 minutes until tender. Add the garlic and sauté 1 minute more. Add the mussels and sauté for 3 minutes, stirring occasionally and gently. Pour in the beer, add the lemon, mustard seed, and herbs and cover the pot.

Steam the mussels until they open, about 5–10 minutes (depending on size). Season with salt and pepper and remove the herb stems before serving.

A favorite dish from the Inn on the Twenty in Ontario. Make sure to serve lots of good crusty bread alongside.
Serves 6.

GEWÜRZTRAMINER-STEAMED MUSSELS

INGREDIENTS

1 Tbsp	grape seed oil	15 mL
1	garlic clove, chopped	1
2	fresh tarragon sprigs	2
½	red onion, finely chopped	½
1	bay leaf	1
1¼ cups	whipping cream (35%)	310 mL
½ cup	Gewürztraminer	125 mL
3 lb	fresh mussels, cleaned	1.5 kg
2	shallots, very finely chopped	2
1 Tbsp	chopped fresh thyme leaves	15 mL
2	celery stalks, trimmed and very finely chopped	2
1	small leek, trimmed, rinsed, and very thinly sliced	1
¾ cup	Gewürztraminer	175 mL
3	plum tomatoes, seeded and chopped	3
1 cup	baby spinach, rinsed and dried	250 mL

METHOD

For the tarragon cream sauce, place a heavy-bottomed pot over low heat. Add the oil, garlic, tarragon, onion, and bay leaf. Sweat the mixture for 5 minutes, or until the onion is soft. Add the cream and wine and cook for another 5 minutes. Remove from the heat and keep the contents warm by placing a lid over the pot.

For the mussels, place a separate heavy-bottomed pot over high heat. Leave on the heat for a few minutes so that the pot is quite hot before adding the mussels.

In a large bowl, combine the mussels, shallots, thyme, celery, and leek. Dump the mussels into the heated pot and immediately pour in the wine; be careful because there will be a lot of steam. Cover the pot and let the mussels cook for 1 minute. Once the mussels begin to open, add the prepared tarragon cream sauce, tomatoes, and spinach. Let cook another minute or until all of the mussels have opened. Discard any that have not opened. Serve immediately.

Spice things up with this saucy combo. Serve this with lots of fresh baguette for dipping, or serve over linguine as a main course. Serves 2 as a main course, 4 as an appetizer.

MUSSELS IN SUN-DRIED TOMATO & CHIPOTLE CREAM SAUCE

INGREDIENTS

2 Tbsp	olive oil	30 mL
⅓ cup	chopped onion or shallots	75 mL
1	garlic clove, minced	1
¼ cup	white wine	60 mL
¼ cup	chopped sun-dried tomatoes (drained if in oil or softened in hot water and drained, if dry)	60 mL
1	chipotle pepper in adobo sauce, minced	1
2 cups	whipping cream (35%)	500 mL
1 cup	milk	250 mL
to taste	salt and freshly ground pepper	to taste
2 tsp	olive oil	10 mL
1½–2 lb	large fresh mussels, cleaned	750 g–1 kg
¼ cup	white wine	60 mL
to taste	Italian parsley, chopped	to taste

METHOD

For the sauce, heat the 2 Tbsp (30 mL) of olive oil over medium heat in a saucepan and add the onion (or shallots) and garlic. Cover and let sweat about 5 minutes.

Add the wine and cook over high heat until reduced. Stir in the sun-dried tomatoes, and add the chipotle, the cream, and milk. Simmer the sauce over medium heat until reduced by about one-third; this should take about 15 minutes. Cool the sauce and purée using a hand blender, until smooth. Adjust the flavor with a little salt and pepper. The sauce may be made ahead to this point and refrigerated.

Heat the 2 tsp (10 mL) of olive oil in a large pan or wok over high heat. When the pan is very hot, add the mussels and toss to coat. Add the wine and toss again. Add the prepared sauce to the pan, toss to coat the mussels, then cover the pan. Reduce to medium-low and simmer, covered, just until the mussels open, about 2–3 minutes. Serve immediately, sprinkled with parsley.

Serving a big bowl of steamed mussels can be a great icebreaker because it's a communal activity. You pass around the bowl and everyone can help themselves. Even if there are guests who don't like mussels, there's always the deliciously garlicky cream to be sopped up with fresh baguette. Serves 6.

MUSSELS
IN GARLIC FENNEL CREAM

INGREDIENTS

2 Tbsp	extra virgin olive oil	30 mL
½ cup	sliced onion	125 mL
1½ cups	thinly sliced fennel bulb	375 mL
3	garlic cloves, thinly sliced	3
2	fresh tarragon sprigs	2
4 lb	fresh mussels, cleaned	1.8 kg
½ cup	white wine	125 mL
1 cup	whipping cream (35%)	250 mL
to taste	coarse salt and ground black pepper	to taste
for dipping	fresh baguette	for dipping

METHOD

Heat a large soup pot over medium-high heat and add the oil. Add the onion and sauté for 1 minute, then add the sliced fennel. Sauté for another 3 minutes then add the garlic and tarragon. Add the mussels and stir to coat. Pour in the white wine and bring to a simmer; then add the whipping cream.

Cover the pot and cook until all the mussels have opened, about 5 minutes. Spoon the mussels into a serving bowl with a slotted spoon. Return the cream to a simmer and season. Remove the tarragon sprigs, pour the cream and vegetables over the mussels, and serve with a fresh baguette.

What makes this mussel preparation unique is the crumbled tortillas that add texture and flavor to the sauce. Making this dish is actually an excuse for me to eat the sauce all by itself. I like to slurp it back with a mussel shell. Serve with bread, warm tortillas, or corn chips. Chipotle chiles en adobo are available in large supermarkets and stores selling Latin American ingredients. Serves 4–6.

SPICY STEAMED MUSSELS
WITH TORTILLA CRUMBS

INGREDIENTS

1 Tbsp	olive oil	15 mL
½ tsp	whole cumin seeds	2 mL
6	garlic cloves, minced	6
½ cup	finely diced onion	125 mL
1	28 oz (796 mL) can plum tomatoes, well drained	1
½ cup	dry red wine	125 mL
2	canned chipotle chiles en adobo, finely chopped	2
pinch	ground allspice	pinch
2	fresh or frozen corn tortillas, crumbled into coarse crumbs	2
3 lb	fresh mussels, cleaned	1.5 kg
¼ cup	coarsely chopped cilantro	60 mL
4	thin slices lime	4

METHOD

Heat the oil in a large, wide, heavy pot over medium-high heat. Add the cumin seeds. When they darken a shade, stir in the garlic and onion and cook until the onion browns lightly. Add the tomato, wine, chilies, and allspice. Simmer over low heat for 10 minutes. The sauce may be prepared up to several hours in advance to this point.

Bring the sauce to a full boil and add the tortillas and mussels. Cover with a lid and steam until the mussels open, about 5–10 minutes. Add the cilantro and lime and shake the pot to distribute the cilantro. Serve immediately in heated bowls.

If you're in a hurry, just pick up some fresh tomato salsa or bruschetta topping at the supermarket to start this speedy dish. Buying farmed mussels will save you time too because they don't require scrubbing or debearding. Serves 2.

ZORBA'S MUSSELS

INGREDIENTS

3 Tbsp	olive oil	45 mL
2	ripe Roma tomatoes, chopped	2
¼ cup	finely chopped red or white onion	60 mL
2	garlic cloves, minced	2
1	green onion, chopped	1
1 Tbsp	chopped Italian parsley	15 mL
1 Tbsp	chopped fresh mint	15 mL
1 tsp	dried basil	5 mL
to taste	salt and freshly ground black pepper	to taste
¼ cup	white wine	60 mL
2–3 lb	fresh mussels, cleaned	1–1.5 kg
2 Tbsp	freshly squeezed lemon juice	30 mL
1–2	thick Greek pita breads, toasted and brushed with garlic butter	1–2

METHOD

In a deep saucepan or wok, heat the olive oil over high heat and sauté the tomato, red onion, and garlic for 5 minutes or until the onion is soft. Add the green onion, parsley, mint, basil, salt, pepper, wine, and the mussels. Cover the pan and steam the mussels, shaking the pan frequently, for 7–8 minutes or until the shells open.

Pour the mussels and pan juices into two shallow soup plates, mounding the mussels high in the serving dishes, and discarding any that don't open. Sprinkle the mussels with lemon juice and serve with thick pita bread that's been toasted and brushed with garlic butter.

My sister-in-law Taw taught me how to prepare green curry sauce. This recipe is a little tamer than hers—Taw likes her food spicy hot and would double the amount of curry paste and add several hot peppers. Serves 6.

MUSSELS

WITH PEPPERS, BAMBOO SHOOTS & GREEN CURRY

INGREDIENTS

1 Tbsp	vegetable oil	15 mL
2 tsp	green curry paste	10 mL
1	14 oz (398 mL) can coconut milk	1
2 Tbsp	Thai fish sauce	30 mL
1 Tbsp	sugar or palm sugar	15 mL
1	kaffir lime leaf (optional)	1
1	small red bell pepper, julienned	1
1	small green bell pepper, julienned	1
1	8 oz (227 g) can sliced bamboo shoots, drained	1
5 lb	fresh mussels, cleaned	2.2 kg
½ cup	chopped fresh Thai basil or sweet basil	125 mL

METHOD

Heat the oil in a large, wide, heavy pot over medium-high heat. Add the curry paste and cook for 1 minute, stirring constantly. Stir in the coconut milk, bring to a boil, and cook for 2 minutes. Add the fish sauce, sugar, kaffir lime leaf, and red and green peppers. Simmer over medium-low heat for 7 minutes. Bring the sauce back to a boil over high heat and add the bamboo shoots and mussels. Cover the pot with a lid and cook until the mussels open, about 5–8 minutes. Stir in the basil. Serve immediately in warm bowls.

Time to put some Edith Piaf on the stereo and serve up a simple but romantic bistro-style meal. Make sure to buy fresh linguine—homemade from an Italian deli or gourmet shop, if possible—or a good artisan-style egg pasta. Like this simple sauce, fresh pasta cooks up almost immediately. Pass a crispy baguette and some sweet butter, and don't forget the champagne, mon amour. *Serves 2.*

FETTUCCINE
WITH MUSSELS & CHERRY TOMATOES

INGREDIENTS

2 Tbsp	olive oil	30 mL
2	shallots, minced	2
2	garlic cloves, minced	2
½ cup	white wine	125 mL
1 cup	grape tomatoes, quartered	250 mL
2 Tbsp	chopped fresh basil	30 mL
1 tsp	finely grated lemon zest	5 mL
to taste	salt and freshly ground black pepper	to taste
¼ cup	whipping cream (35%)	60 mL
2 lb	fresh mussels, cleaned	1 kg
½ lb	fresh fettuccine	250 g

METHOD

Bring a large pot of salted water to a boil.

Meanwhile, in a large, deep saucepan, heat the olive oil over high heat and sauté the shallots and garlic for 3 minutes. Add the white wine, bring to a boil, and simmer until the wine is reduced by half.

Stir in the tomatoes, half of the basil, the lemon zest, and salt and pepper. Add the cream and simmer for 2–3 minutes. Add the mussels to the pan, and cover and shake for about 2–3 minutes or until the shells open. Remove the pan from the heat and set aside, discarding any shells that haven't opened.

Add the pasta to the boiling water. Boil until the pasta is al dente, then drain and return to the cooking pot. Pour the mussels and sauce over the cooked pasta and toss to combine. Divide the pasta and sauce between two warm soup plates or pasta bowls, arranging the mussels overtop. Sprinkle with the remaining basil and serve immediately.

SCALLOPS

Frankly scallop, I don't give a clam!

—Pinkard and Bowden, "I Lobster but Never Flounder"

❧

MY FAMILY WERE NOT BIG SHELLFISH EATERS. There was always a can of shrimp in the cupboard, and if I had eaten it, my memory of eating it is vague. It was probably one of those cans that sat in the cupboard for years, becoming an expected part of the pantry landscape.

So when I was young, I wondered about scallops. Specifically, I wondered what scalloped potatoes and scallops had in common. The Shell gasoline station had a scallop shell as its logo. I would look at the sign and try to relate it to scalloped potatoes. The shell looked sort of layered and maybe that was the similarity. I had learned in school that our ancestors had tools and knives made from shells, bones, and wood. So, maybe scalloped potatoes were originally cut with a scallop shell because it certainly looked like it could do the job. This explanation seemed to satisfy me and I didn't think about scallops for many years until I finally ate one. Now I don't know which is better: scallops or scalloped potatoes.

In addition to its luxurious taste and texture, the scallop is also known for its beautiful shell. Most people are probably familiar with Botticelli's *Birth of Venus*, which depicts the Roman goddess Venus on a scallop shell. Buildings in ancient Pompeii were decorated with scallop shell ornaments.

What exactly is the scallop that we like to eat? Scallops are bivalves with two-hinged shells. They differ from oysters, clams, and mussels in their ability to swim short distances by opening and closing their shells rapidly. On the West Coast, we sometimes hear the term "swimming scallop" because of this unique ability. As a result, scallops develop an oversized muscle referred to as the *scallop adductor*, which is what we eat.

Scallops are primarily harvested by dredging and are shucked soon after capture. They are shucked on board the ships and refrigerated or frozen.

Storing and Preparing Scallops

It's rare to find fresh scallop meat; most is frozen, and then thawed for retail sale. Raw scallops should have a firm texture and a sweet and mild scent. They should have a creamy, off-white appearance. Some female sea scallops may have a slight orange color, which does not affect the taste or texture. Scallops that look too evenly shaped or too white in color may have been soaked in a sodium tripolyphosphate (STPP) solution. This preservative plumps up the meat, making the scallops look larger and whiter. When these scallops are cooked, they exude water and end up being small and tough with a soapy aftertaste. Beware the bargain scallop!

Store scallops refrigerated and covered. On the side of each scallop, you'll see a small tendon which should be removed by hand before cooking since it's a little on the chewy side. Dry scallops thoroughly before frying or searing as the moisture will inhibit browning. I think scallops are best cooked at high temperature and medium rare, which will keep them moist and succulent. When cooking, don't shake the pan because the scallops will split. Turn them gently with tongs.

The sweetness of the peas is a good complement to the tangy scallops. Serves 6.

CHILLED SUGAR SNAP PEA SOUP
WITH MARINATED SCALLOPS

INGREDIENTS

10–12	small (or 4–6 large) scallops	10–12
1 Tbsp	extra virgin olive oil	15 mL
1 Tbsp	lime juice	15 mL
½ tsp	lime zest	2 mL
to taste	salt and freshly ground black pepper	to taste
1–2 Tbsp	vegetable oil	15–30 mL
1	large onion, diced	1
1 Tbsp	sugar	15 mL
1 cup	dry white wine	250 mL
6 cups	chicken stock or water	1.5 L
1	bay leaf	1
4	fresh thyme sprigs, tied in string	4
1 tsp	salt	5 mL
1½ lb	sugar snap peas	750 g
to taste	salt and freshly ground black pepper	to taste

METHOD

Dice the scallops very finely. Toss with the olive oil, lime juice, and zest. Season with salt and pepper. Keep refrigerated until ready to serve.

Heat the vegetable oil over medium-high heat. Add the onion and sweat gently until translucent and very soft. Add the sugar and cook for 1 minute. Add the wine and simmer for 5–10 minutes. Add the chicken stock, bay leaf, and thyme sprigs. Simmer for 20 minutes.

Strain the stock, discarding the onion, bay leaf, and thyme sprigs, and bring it to a boil. Add 1 tsp (5 mL) salt. To blanch the peas, add to the boiling stock, cooking until they just begin to soften. Strain out the peas immediately, retaining the stock, and plunge the peas quickly into ice water. Drain as soon as they have cooled. Chill the reserved stock. When cold, purée the peas with the stock. Strain. Season with salt and pepper.

To serve, ladle the soup into chilled bowls. Spoon the scallops into the center of each bowl.

You will love the color and texture of this ceviche as well as the combination of fresh seafood with tropical tastes. When making ceviche, it is important to use very fresh fish as it is never cooked by heat, only by acids contained in citrus juice. Serve this dish immediately. If left standing, the flavors meld together and become indistinguishable. Makes 6 generous appetizers.

TUNA & SCALLOP CEVICHE
WITH TROPICAL FRUITS

INGREDIENTS

12 oz	fresh or fresh-frozen scallops, thinly sliced	375 g
12 oz	sashimi-grade tuna, thinly sliced	375 g
2–4	limes, juice only	2–4
1	small pink grapefruit	1
1	mango	1
2 Tbsp	light soy sauce or tamari (wheat-free soy sauce)	30 mL
3 Tbsp	finely chopped fresh coriander	45 mL
¼ tsp	sesame oil	1 mL
¼–½ tsp	finely minced jalapeño pepper	1–2 mL

METHOD

Toss the scallops and tuna with the lime juice in two separate bowls and let sit for 10 minutes. Meanwhile, peel and section the grapefruit, cutting around the membrane. Dice the grapefruit. Peel and slice the mango into ¼-inch (6 mm) slices.

Drain the scallops and the tuna, reserving the lime juice. In a bowl, gently toss them together and then toss with the soy sauce, coriander, sesame oil, and jalapeño pepper. When the fish is thoroughly coated, fold in the grapefruit and mango. Taste, and add some of the reserved lime juice, if necessary.

Using your hands, mound on six plates and serve immediately.

Scallops the size of hockey pucks are available, but for this recipe I use ones that are about 1 inch (2.5 cm) across. I like to cook scallops to a medium doneness, but you have to watch that they don't overcook and become rubbery. Serves 4.

HOT SCALLOP SALAD

WITH BUTTER LETTUCE, MUSTARD, TARRAGON & SHERRY

INGREDIENTS

3 Tbsp	olive oil	45 mL
16	scallops	16
¼ cup	minced onion	60 mL
1 tsp	minced garlic	5 mL
4 tsp	Dijon mustard	20 mL
4 tsp	grainy mustard	20 mL
4 tsp	chopped fresh tarragon	20 mL
½ cup	dry sherry	125 mL
½ cup	whipping cream (35%)	125 mL
½ tsp	salt	2 mL
½ tsp	black pepper	2 mL
1	head butter lettuce	1

METHOD

Heat the oil in a sauté pan over medium heat. Add the scallops and cook for about 1 minute on each side. Remove from the pan. Add the onion, garlic, mustards, and tarragon to the pan. Add the sherry. When the mixture comes to a boil, add the cream, salt, and pepper. Cook until it reduces by half. Return the scallops to the pan and remove from the heat.

Cut the lettuce in quarters and place each piece in the middle of a plate. Pour the scallop mixture overtop and serve immediately.

Spring roll wrappers and wasabi powder can be found in the Asian food section of almost any supermarket. When making the spring rolls, cover the remaining wrappers with a slightly damp towel to prevent drying. Serves 4.

SCALLOP & GREEN ONION SPRING ROLLS

WITH WASABI MAYONNAISE

INGREDIENTS

Filling

10 oz	bay scallops	300 g
2	green onions, thinly sliced	2
1 Tbsp	mayonnaise	15 mL
1 tsp	grainy mustard	5 mL
2 tsp	chopped fresh basil	10 mL
pinch	sea salt and freshly ground black pepper	pinch

Wasabi Mayonnaise

1 Tbsp	wasabi powder	15 mL
3 Tbsp	whipping cream (35%)	45 mL
½ cup	mayonnaise	125 mL
1 Tbsp	chopped fresh basil	15 mL
1 Tbsp	lemon juice	15 mL

Assembly

1	¾ lb (340 g) package spring roll wrappers	1
1	egg, slightly beaten	1
for frying	canola oil	for frying

METHOD

To prepare the filling, blot the scallops with a paper towel to soak up any excess moisture. Roughly chop them and place in a small mixing bowl. Add the green onions, 1 Tbsp (15 mL) mayonnaise, mustard, 2 tsp (10 mL) basil, and salt and pepper and mix with a wooden spoon to combine. Refrigerate until needed.

In a separate bowl, whisk the wasabi powder into the whipping cream. Add the ½ cup (125 mL) mayonnaise, 1 Tbsp (15 mL) basil, and lemon juice. Whisk to combine and set aside. Refrigerate until needed.

Working with one at a time, lay out the spring roll wrapper diagonally and brush the part farthest away from you with a little egg. Place approximately 3 Tbsp (45 mL) of the filling onto the wrapper. Starting with the point closest to you, roll it up over the filling. Fold each side point towards the center and continue to roll away from you to form a small cylinder-shaped spring roll. Repeat with the remaining filling.

Place about 3 inches (8 mm) of canola oil in a pot that is at least 6 inches (15 cm) deep and heat to 375°F (190°C). Fry the spring rolls for about 5 minutes, or until golden brown. Serve hot, with the wasabi mayonnaise on the side for dipping.

This is a beautiful dish—the light-colored scallops play off against the dark colors of the glaze. Recommended wine: Chenin Blanc—a medium-bodied, medium-acidity wine with a honey, candied fruit flavor. Serves 6–8 as an appetizer.

SCALLOPS

WITH CHINESE MAHOGANY GLAZE

INGREDIENTS

1 lb	large scallops	500 g
1 cup	hoisin sauce	250 mL
¾ cup	plum sauce	175 mL
½ cup	light soy sauce	125 mL
⅓ cup	wine vinegar	75 mL
¼ cup	dry sherry	60 mL
¼ cup	honey	60 mL
½ cup	minced green onion	125 mL
6	garlic cloves, finely minced	6
2 Tbsp	finely minced ginger	30 mL
¼ cup	toasted white sesame seeds	60 mL

METHOD

Combine all the ingredients in a nonreactive bowl and marinate the scallops for 30 minutes.

Drain the marinade into a pan and cook until it is reduced to the consistency of a thick sauce.

Cook the scallops on a hot grill for about 3 minutes, until they just begin to feel firm when prodded with your finger. Serve at once, drizzled with the reduced marinade.

Since you've probably already popped the cork, save some champagne for this simple sauce. Steam some baby vegetables to serve on the side or serve it in a nest of fresh angel hair pasta. Love at first bite and a complete meal for two. Serves 2.

SEARED SCALLOPS
IN CHAMPAGNE SAUCE

INGREDIENTS

¾ cup	brut (dry) champagne	175 mL
2	shallots, minced	2
2 Tbsp	whipping cream (35%)	30 mL
4 Tbsp	cold butter, cut into small cubes	60 mL
½ lb	fresh angel hair pasta	250 g
1 tsp	butter	5 mL
1 tsp	olive oil	5 mL
¾ lb	large sea scallops	375 g
to taste	salt and white pepper	to taste
2 Tbsp	chopped chives	30 mL

METHOD

In a small saucepan, combine the champagne and shallots and bring to a boil over high heat. Cook for 15–20 minutes, until the liquid has been reduced to only a tablespoon or two. Remove from the heat, and whisk in the whipping cream and the cubed butter, a few cubes at a time. Return the pan to low heat and continue whisking until all the butter has been added. The sauce should emulsify. Remove from the heat.

Meanwhile, cook the pasta in plenty of boiling, salted water until al dente. Drain and keep warm.

Heat 1 tsp (5 mL) of butter and the olive oil in a heavy, nonstick pan over high heat. Add the scallops and sear until they are golden, about 2–3 minutes on each side. The scallops should be nearly rare inside and caramelized outside. Season with salt and pepper.

On two warm plates, arrange the seared scallops on a nest of hot pasta. Drizzle with the sauce and sprinkle with chopped chives.

The mildness of apricots brings out a natural sweetness in the scallops, which can be further complemented by serving an off-dry Riesling. Sea salt is added after the scallops have been cooked, to avoid drawing out juices while cooking. If you can't find large scallops (under 10 per pound), double the amount. Serves 6.

SCALLOPS
ON APRICOT BUTTER SAUCE

INGREDIENTS

1	shallot, minced	1
4	fresh apricots, pitted and diced	4
²/₃ cup	white wine	150 mL
1	lemon, juice of	1
½ cup	unsalted butter, cut into small pieces and chilled	125 mL
to taste	salt and pepper	to taste
½ tsp	sugar or honey	2 mL
2 Tbsp	vegetable oil	30 mL
18	large fresh scallops	18
to taste	sea salt and pepper	to taste

METHOD

To make the sauce, place the shallot, apricots, wine, and lemon juice in a small saucepan and simmer until the liquid is reduced by half. Reduce the heat to low and gradually add the cold butter, a piece at a time while stirring, until all the butter is incorporated. Season with salt and pepper and sugar or honey. Remove from the heat and set aside.

To make the scallops, place a heavy-bottomed or cast iron skillet on medium-high heat. Wait until the pan begins to smoke slightly then add the oil to coat the bottom of the pan. Add the scallops carefully. Sear the scallops in multiple batches if you need to, to avoid overcrowding. After 1 minute, loosen the scallops from the bottom of the pan using tongs or a spatula. Continue to cook over high heat for 1 minute. Turn the scallops over and sear for an additional 2 minutes.

To serve, spoon some sauce onto each plate, arrange 3 scallops on top, and season with salt and pepper.

Searing scallops in a very hot pan and cooking them quickly in the sauce is essential in this recipe. If the pan is not hot enough, the scallops will not caramelize on the bottom and they will shrink and get tough. The whisky and basil create an incredible aroma that is infused into the scallops. Serves 4.

WHISKY & COCONUT MARINATED SCALLOPS

INGREDIENTS

1	clove garlic, minced	1
⅛ tsp	crushed white pepper	0.5 mL
6 Tbsp	whisky	90 mL
3 Tbsp	coconut cream	45 mL
1 Tbsp	red curry paste	15 mL
1 lb	large scallops	500 g
2 tsp	vegetable oil	10 mL
½ cup	coconut milk	125 mL
1 tsp	palm sugar	5 mL
2 tsp	fish sauce	10 mL
½ cup	sliced green onions	125 mL
3 Tbsp	chopped fresh basil	45 mL

METHOD

In a medium-sized bowl, combine the garlic, pepper, 3 Tbsp (45 mL) of the whisky, coconut cream, and curry paste. Add the scallops, toss to coat, and marinate for 15 minutes.

Heat the oil in a heavy skillet until it's almost smoking. Add the scallops and stir-fry for 1–2 minutes. Lower the heat to medium and add the coconut milk, sugar, fish sauce, remaining 3 Tbsp (45 mL) whisky, green onions, and basil. Cook for 1 more minute.

TIP

For the coconut cream, use the thick, rich cream that is at the top of the can of coconut milk.

Scallops taste almost sweet and pair well with tropical flavors. This combination of mango, lime, and ginger brings one of my favorite mollusks to delicious new heights. Serve with steamed rice and stir-fried vegetables. Serves 4.

PAN-SEARED SCALLOPS
ON GINGER-SPIKED MANGO SAUCE

INGREDIENTS

1	medium ripe mango, peeled and coarsely chopped	1
2 tsp	freshly grated ginger	10 mL
2 Tbsp	lime juice	30 mL
2 tsp	brown sugar	10 mL
pinch	crushed chili flakes	pinch
¼ cup	water	60 mL
20	large sea scallops	20
1 tsp	ground cumin	5 mL
to taste	salt and white pepper	to taste
2 Tbsp	olive oil	30 mL
2 Tbsp	fresh lime juice	30 mL
4	cilantro sprigs and lime slices	4

METHOD

To make the mango sauce, place the mango, ginger, the 2 Tbsp (30 mL) of lime juice, brown sugar, chili flakes, and water in a food processor or blender and purée until smooth. Transfer to a small pot and gently simmer over medium heat for 10 minutes. Keep warm over low heat while you cook the scallops.

Season the scallops with the cumin, salt, and pepper. Heat the oil in a nonstick skillet over high heat. Cook the scallops for 1–2 minutes per side, or until just cooked through. Sprinkle with lime juice and remove from the heat. Spoon the mango sauce on 4 plates. Arrange the scallops on top. Garnish with cilantro and lime.

OPTION

For curried mango sauce, omit the crushed chili flakes from the sauce and add curry paste or powder to taste before simmering the sauce.

If you have square wrappers, cut them into rounds with a cookie cutter or just make triangular dumplings.
Makes 40.

SHRIMP & SCALLOP DUMPLINGS
WITH SOY CHILI DIP

INGREDIENTS

½ lb	bay or sea scallops	250 g
½ lb	peeled and deveined raw shrimp	250 g
1	egg white	1
4	green onions, minced	4
6	water chestnuts, minced	6
1 Tbsp	dry sherry or sake	15 mL
1 Tbsp	light soy sauce	15 mL
1 tsp	sesame oil	5 mL
½ tsp	salt	2 mL
2 tsp	grated fresh ginger	10 mL
1	garlic clove, crushed	1
2 tsp	cornstarch	10 mL
40	wonton wrappers or dumpling skins	40

Dipping Sauce

2 Tbsp	light soy sauce	30 mL
1 Tbsp	rice vinegar	15 mL
1 tsp	Asian chili paste	5 mL
1	green onion, minced	1

METHOD

In a food processor, combine the scallops, shrimp, and the egg white. Pulse several times to coarsely chop the seafood (don't purée, just chop). Add the green onions, chestnuts, sherry, soy sauce, sesame oil, salt, ginger, garlic, and cornstarch. Pulse again, just to combine.

To fill the wontons, place a generous 1 tsp (5 mL) portion of filling on each wrapper. Use your finger to moisten the edges of the wrapper with water, then fold over, pressing the edges to seal. Dust a tray with cornstarch and the dumplings on the tray. Cover and refrigerate until you're ready to cook them.

To make the dipping sauce, whisk together the soy sauce, rice vinegar, chili paste, and green onion in a small bowl. Set aside.

To cook the dumplings, bring 12 cups (3 L) of water to a boil. Add half the dumplings, stirring gently to prevent them from sticking together. The dumplings are cooked when they rise to the top and float for about 20 seconds. Remove the cooked dumplings from the water with a slotted spoon and drain. Serve the dumplings immediately with the dipping sauce.

If you prefer pan-fried dumplings, heat 3 Tbsp (45 mL) of oil in a nonstick skillet over medium-high heat and arrange the dumplings, packed tightly together, sealed side up, in the oil. Fry them until golden brown on the bottom, then add 1 cup (250 mL) of water to the pan. Bring to a boil and cover. Reduce the heat to low, and cook for 10 minutes. Uncover, pour out the water, and return the pan to medium heat. Drizzle with 1½ tsp (7 mL) of oil and fry for 2 minutes longer to crisp. Invert the dumplings onto a platter, golden side up, and serve with dipping sauce.

Wrapping scallops in prosciutto offers a more intriguing, Italian-style taste, and is a little less fatty alternative to streaky bacon. Serves 4 as an appetizer, 2 as a main course.

PROSCIUTTO-WRAPPED SCALLOPS

WITH PESTO MAYONNAISE

INGREDIENTS

½ cup	mayonnaise	125 mL
2 Tbsp	pesto (homemade or store bought)	30 mL
to taste	salt, white pepper, and lemon juice	to taste
12	large scallops	12
6	paper-thin slices prosciutto, each cut in half lengthwise	6

METHOD

Combine the mayonnaise, pesto, salt and pepper, and lemon juice in a small bowl. Cover and set aside in the fridge. Preheat the oven to 425°F (220°C).

Wrap a half piece of prosciutto around the outer edge of each scallop. Secure with a toothpick, if necessary. Place on a nonstick or parchment-lined baking sheet. Bake for 8–10 minutes, or until just cooked through. Arrange on appetizer plates or a platter, with a bowl of the mayonnaise alongside for dipping.

Scallops and foie gras have become a classic pairing. The red wine risotto makes it divine. Makes 6 appetizer servings.

SCALLOPS
WITH FOIE GRAS & RED WINE RISOTTO

INGREDIENTS

6	sea scallops	6
to taste	kosher salt and white pepper	to taste
6 oz	fresh foie gras, divided into 6 portions	175 g

METHOD

Season the scallops with salt and pepper. Place a large sauté pan over high heat. Season the foie gras with salt and pepper and add to the hot pan. Sear the foie gras until golden brown on each side, about 1 minute per side. Remove from the heat and transfer to a plate with kitchen towels to absorb excess fat.

Pour the excess fat out of the sauté pan and return the pan to high heat. Add the scallops and cook on one side only until crispy brown, about 2 minutes. Remove from the heat and keep warm while you prepare the risotto.

Red Wine Risotto

2 cups	Merlot	500 mL
4 cups	chicken stock	1 L
2 Tbsp	unsalted butter	30 mL
2	shallots, finely chopped	2
1 tsp	minced garlic	5 mL
1 cup	arborio rice	250 mL
1 cup	fava beans, peeled and blanched	250 mL
2 Tbsp	grated Parmesan cheese	30 mL
to taste	kosher salt and pepper	to taste

Place the Merlot in a small saucepan over medium heat and reduce until only 2 Tbsp (30 mL) of wine remains. Set aside.

Bring the chicken stock to a rapid boil.

In a large sauté pan over medium heat, melt the butter with the shallots. Sauté the shallots until soft, about 5 minutes. Add the garlic, stir for 2 minutes, then stir in the arborio rice.

Using a small ladle, transfer the boiling chicken stock to the rice. Stir until all of the stock has been absorbed. Continue to stir for 18–20 minutes, or until the rice is just cooked through and creamy.

Remove from the heat and fold in the fava beans, Parmesan, and salt and pepper. Using a rubber spatula, scrape the red wine reduction into the risotto and blend.

Divide the risotto among 6 warm dinner plates and top with the seared scallops. Place a piece of seared foie gras on each scallop and serve.

We've been making this appetizer for years. The delicate flavors are beautifully balanced—fit to impress anyone, but most importantly, you. When searing scallops, it's better to sear just a few at a time, leaving space between them. Overcrowding the pan just cools it down and the scallops will sweat out their juices. Serves 2.

SCALLOPS WITH LEMON RISOTTO

INGREDIENTS

Sweet Lemon Garnish

2 Tbsp	lemon marmalade	30 mL
1 Tbsp	white wine	15 mL
2 Tbsp	finely diced red bell pepper	30 mL

Lemon Risotto

1 Tbsp	extra virgin olive oil	15 mL
2 Tbsp	minced onion	30 mL
¼ cup	Arborio or Carnaroli rice	60 mL
2 Tbsp	white wine	30 mL
1½ tsp	finely grated lemon zest	7 mL
pinch	Spanish saffron	pinch
1½ cups	water	375 mL
1 Tbsp	fresh lemon juice	15 mL
2 Tbsp	unsalted butter	30 mL
1 tsp	honey	5 mL
to taste	coarse salt	to taste

Scallops

6	fresh scallops	6
to taste	coarse sea salt and ground black pepper	to taste
1 Tbsp	extra virgin olive oil	15 mL

Recipe continues on page 96 . . .

METHOD

To make the lemon garnish, heat the marmalade over medium-low heat with the white wine and diced red pepper until the pepper softens. Remove from the heat and chill until ready to serve, but allow to come up to room temperature for serving.

To make the lemon risotto, heat the olive oil in a heavy-bottomed saucepan over medium heat and add the onion, stirring until translucent, about 5 minutes, reducing the heat if any browning occurs. Add the rice and stir for another 3 minutes to coat the rice with oil. Add the white wine all at once and stir until absorbed. Stir in the lemon zest and saffron and add the water, about ½ cup (125 mL) at a time, stirring after each addition and then stirring frequently (but no need to stir constantly), adding the next addition of water only after the previous one has been fully absorbed. Check the doneness of rice by tasting (remember that it will continue cooking once removed from heat). The cooking process should only take about 18–20 minutes, as it is such a small amount of rice. Set aside while preparing the scallops.

To make the scallops, remove them from the fridge when starting the risotto, to bring them to room temperature. Heat a large, nonstick sauté pan over high heat and add the oil. Season both sides of the scallops and place in the pan, leaving a 1-inch (2.5 cm) space between them. Jiggle the scallops slightly with a pair of tongs to loosen and cook 3 minutes on each side.

To serve, finish the risotto by adding the lemon juice, butter, honey, and salt and pepper to taste and heat for a minute. Spoon the risotto onto 2 plates and arrange 3 scallops on top of the risotto. Top with a spoonful of lemon marmalade and serve immediately.

SHRIMP & PRAWNS

Anyway, like I was sayin', shrimp is the fruit of the sea.

You can barbecue it, boil it, broil it, bake it, sauté it.

Dey's uh . . . shrimp kabobs, shrimp creole, shrimp gumbo.

Pan fried, deep fried, stir-fried. There's pineapple shrimp, lemon

shrimp, coconut shrimp, pepper shrimp, shrimp soup, shrimp stew,

shrimp salad, shrimp and potatoes, shrimp burger, shrimp

sandwich. That, that's about it.

—from *Forrest Gump*

∽

ONE OF MY FONDEST FOOD MEMORIES IS EATING FRESHLY CAUGHT, COOKED SHRIMP AT A ROADSIDE STAND ON THE GULF OF ST. LAWRENCE. They were in the shell, complete with their heads. The same stand also sold hand-cut french fries. I was almost giddy, eating my first real shrimp with real french fries. At that time, which was 30 years ago, they were $1.50 per pound. Moving to the West Coast 20 years later, I was happy to find that the Spot prawn matched my experience on the East Coast. In between I've had many shrimp and prawns, all over the world.

What's the Difference?

There is a great deal of confusion about what a *shrimp* is and what a *prawn* is; both terms are used to describe several different shellfish. A lot of the confusion is within North America; on the East Coast, these crustaceans are called shrimp, and on the West Coast, they're called prawns. For some reason, West Coast folks think that shrimp are small, and prawns are large. When I first moved to Vancouver, arguments would break out over the terms so I stopped fighting and just gave in. (West Coasters also think that cilantro is the fresh herb and coriander refers to seed, which is incorrect also. But, I digress.)

These terms have nothing to do with size, but with species. Without getting too technical, shrimp are distinguished from prawns by the structure of the gills.

The tiger shrimp you buy in Toronto are the same as the tiger prawns you buy in Vancouver. The West Coast Spot prawn is actually a shrimp, and the beat goes on . . . I've invented a new word to deal with the confusion: *shrawn*. Or maybe that should be *primp*?

The most commonly available black tiger shrimp or prawn is easily recognizable by the dark stripes on its shell. Of all shrimp, these are among the most widely distributed and marketed in the world. Almost all of the black tigers on the market are farmed in Asia. In fact, most of the prawns available here are black tiger, although you can sometimes find the stripeless white shrimp. They are always frozen, and except for the largest sizes, headless. Most retailers will have them conveniently thawed in the display case.

Even on the West Coast, the local Spot prawns are not readily available, and when they are, the price is prohibitive for a lot of people. In some areas, they can be bought fresh off the boat, and a few retailers—mostly in the Asian sector—have live tanks with Spot prawns swimming about. People who enjoy these prawns like to get quite personal with what they are eating. You can't be squeamish when presented with a bag of live, squirming prawns that have to be trimmed and cooked. Consider me part of the group of nonsqueamish eaters. I find that these prawns are best cooked in the shell with the head on (once the legs and feelers have been trimmed). Inside the head is a creamy yellow "fat" that whole-prawn eaters relish. Some sushi restaurants have live tanks, and you can enjoy the prawn as sushi or sashimi. The head is whisked off to the kitchen and returned to your side deep-fried, crunchy and delicious.

The East Coast fishery is a little different from that in the West Coast, having an inshore and an offshore component. Inshore boats that fish the Gulf of St. Lawrence, on the Scotian Shelf, and off northwestern Newfoundland deliver fresh and frozen shrimp to shore plants for cooking and peeling. The offshore fishery has large factory ships capable of cooking and freezing shrimp within minutes of harvest. On the West Coast they are fished close to shore by one-man beam trawls or otter trawls. Most are day boats with a few larger vessels fishing for three days at a stretch.

In the recipes featured in this chapter, small and cooked crustaceans have been termed "cooked baby shrimp." *Shrimp* or *prawn* is used elsewhere, meaning raw and headless, and the size you'll need is specified.

So whether you enjoy shrimp or prawns, or both, one thing is certain: they're delicious, readily available, and easy to cook. So let's get started . . .

Shrimp and Prawn Sizing Guide

Shrimp and prawns are graded by number per pound. The lower the number, the larger they are, with less units per pound. The "U" in U/10, U/12, and U/15 means "under." There are less than 10 pieces, 12 pieces, and 15 pieces respectively per pound.

Size	Number per pound	Average number	
		per pound	per 4 oz serving
Extra Colossal	U/10	5	3
Colossal	U/12	9	3
Colossal	U/15	14	4
Extra Jumbo	16/20	18	5
Jumbo	21/25	23	6
Extra Large	26/30	28	7
Large	31/35	33	8
Medium Large	36/40	38	10
Medium	41/50	45	12
Small	51/60	55	14
Extra Small	61/70	65	16

Peeling Shrimp and Prawns

There are gadgets on the market for peeling shrimp and prawns. You insert a prong under the shell and it is supposed to magically fly off, deveining the prawn at the same time. Save your money because none of them work as well as shelling them by hand. With your thumb and forefinger, pinch the underside of the shell where the legs are. Peel the shell up and away from you. Try both ways, starting from the top down or the bottom up. You'll find one or the other easier. The shell is segmented, so pinching as many segments as you can at one time will speed up the process.

The easy way of doing this is to buy the prawns already shelled and cleaned—although it makes the soup a little lighter in flavor. Otherwise, you can cook the prawn shells together with the spices for about 10 minutes, then take the shells out and cook with the chicken stock. You need lots of crusty bread with this. Serves 6 as a generous appetizer.

PRAWN & PEANUT SOUP
WITH LIME & COCONUT

INGREDIENTS

2 Tbsp	unsalted butter	30 mL
1½ lb	extra-large prawns (26/30)	750 g
1	large onion, chopped	1
6	garlic cloves, chopped	6
2–3	hot chilies, minced	2–3
2 Tbsp	minced fresh ginger	30 mL
4 cups	chicken stock or water, or combination	1 L
2	14 oz (398 mL) cans Italian diced tomatoes	2
1	14 oz (398 mL) can unsweetened coconut milk	1
½ cup	peanut butter (creamy is better than chunky)	125 mL
½ cup	fresh lime juice (juice of 5 or 6 limes)	125 mL
to taste	chopped cilantro	to taste
to taste	salt and pepper	to taste

METHOD

Melt the butter in a good-sized soup kettle or pot. Add the prawns, onion, garlic, chilies, and ginger and cook for 2 minutes.

Take out the prawns with a slotted spoon. Add the chicken stock or water and simmer for 10 minutes. Stir in the tomatoes and simmer 10 minutes more.

Mix together the coconut milk and peanut butter until smooth (use a hand mixer, whisk, or food processor). Stir this mixture into the broth.

Add the prawns, lime juice, and cilantro. Simmer gently to heat through, 2–3 minutes. Season with salt and pepper and serve with chopped cilantro and slices of lime on top.

Tom Yam (spicy fragrant soup) is the most famous soup in Thai cuisine. It has all the defining flavors of a traditional dish—lemongrass, chili, lime, kaffir lime leaf, galangal, garlic. But the real key to the flavor in this dish is the stock made from the prawn shells. Whenever I peel prawns I throw the shells into the freezer until I have enough to make a big batch of prawn stock. Serves 6.

TOM YAM PRAWN SOUP

INGREDIENTS

¾ lb	large prawns (31/35)	375 g
1 tsp	oil	5 mL
3 cups	chicken or fish stock	750 mL
2 cups	water	500 mL
3	stalks lemongrass, cut in ½-inch (1 cm) slices	3
5	kaffir lime leaves	5
2	small red chili peppers, sliced	2
1	garlic clove, minced	1
1	1-inch (2.5 cm) piece galangal, sliced	1
1 cup	sliced mushrooms	250 mL
½	onion, thinly sliced	½
1	celery stalk, thinly sliced	1
1	red bell pepper, thinly sliced	1
2	limes, juiced	2
1 Tbsp	fish sauce	15 mL
3	green onions, sliced	3
¼ cup	chopped cilantro leaves and stems	60 mL

METHOD

Remove the shells from the prawns, saving the shells. Slice the prawns in half lengthwise and refrigerate.

In a large pot, heat the oil and sauté the prawn shells until pink. Add the stock, water, lemongrass, lime leaves, chili peppers, garlic, and galangal. Bring to a boil. Lower the heat, cover, and simmer for 60 minutes.

Strain the stock mixture and return it to the pot. Bring to a boil and add the mushrooms, onion, celery, and red pepper. Reduce the heat and simmer for 2 minutes.

Add the prawns and simmer for another 2 minutes. Add the lime juice, fish sauce, green onion, and cilantro just before serving.

Pimentone is smoked paprika, a spice that goes particularly well with creamy seafood dishes. Serves 12.

CORN CHOWDER
WITH SEARED PIMENTONE SHRIMP

INGREDIENTS

3 Tbsp	unsalted butter	45 mL
1 cup	diced onion	250 mL
1 cup	diced celery	250 mL
2 cups	diced potatoes	500 mL
½ cup	diced carrots	125 mL
½ cup	diced red pepper	125 mL
½ tsp	saffron	2 mL
6 cups	fresh corn kernels	1.5 L
3 Tbsp	all-purpose flour	45 mL
8 cups	chicken stock	2 L
to taste	salt and freshly ground black pepper	to taste
½ cup	10% cream	125 mL
4 Tbsp	finely chopped fresh cilantro	60 mL
1½ lb	jumbo shrimp (21/25), shelled and cut in half lengthwise	750 g
2 Tbsp	olive oil	30 mL
1 Tbsp	pimentone or smoked paprika	15 mL

METHOD

In a large pot over medium heat, melt the butter and sauté the onion, celery, potatoes, carrots, and peppers until the onion is translucent. Add the saffron and corn and cook for 1 minute. Add the flour and stir to form a roux. Slowly whisk in the chicken stock, and bring to a boil over medium heat.

Reduce heat, add the salt and pepper, cream, and cilantro, and simmer for 20 minutes until the potatoes are tender.

Meanwhile, marinate the shrimp in a mixture of olive oil and pimentone. Season with salt and pepper. Sauté the shrimp over high heat, just until cooked. Garnish each bowl of soup with some shrimp and serve at once.

I like to serve this soup to start off a spring dinner when fresh, local asparagus is at its finest. Serves 4.

SHRIMP & ASPARAGUS SOUP

INGREDIENTS

3 Tbsp	olive oil	45 mL
¾ lb	asparagus, trimmed and sliced	375 g
½	medium onion, sliced	½
3 Tbsp	all-purpose flour	45 mL
4 cups	fish, chicken, or vegetable stock	1 L
⅓ lb	cooked salad shrimp, plus some to garnish	170 g
1 Tbsp	chopped fresh tarragon or dill	15 mL
½ cup	whipping cream (35%)	125 mL
to taste	salt and white pepper	to taste
to garnish	tarragon or parsley sprigs	to garnish

METHOD

Heat the oil in a pot over medium heat. Add the asparagus and onion and cook, stirring, for 4–5 minutes. Mix in the flour until well combined. Slowly pour in the stock, whisking steadily, until all is combined. Bring to a simmer and cook until the asparagus is very tender, about 20 minutes.

Purée the mixture in a food processor or blender, and then return to the pot. Bring back to a gentle simmer, and then stir in the shrimp, tarragon or dill, and cream. Cook for 5 minutes more. Ladle the soup into bowls. Decorate the top of each serving with a few shrimp and a tarragon or parsley sprig.

OPTION

To make crab or lobster and asparagus soup, simply replace the shrimp with an equal amount of crabmeat or thinly sliced cooked lobster.

PHOTO BY TRACY KUSIEWICZ • FOOD STYLING BY IRENE MCGUINESS

The crispness of the bread, the creaminess of the avocado, and the crunch of the shrimp make a mouthwatering combination. If you can't find the chipotle and ancho peppers, substitute chili or cayenne pepper to taste. You can prepare all the components ahead of time and serve cool, but I prefer the taste of these crostini when the bread and shrimp are still warm. Makes 12 pieces.

GRILLED SHRIMP & AVOCADO BUTTER CROSTINI

INGREDIENTS

1	lime, juice of	1
1	avocado, peeled, pit removed	1
1 Tbsp	finely minced onion	15 mL
1/8 tsp	kosher salt	0.5 mL
1/8 tsp	freshly ground white pepper	0.5 mL
1/8 tsp	chipotle pepper, or to taste	0.5 mL
1/8 tsp	ancho pepper, or to taste	0.5 mL
2 tsp	shredded fresh basil	10 mL
1/2 cup	vegetable or canola oil	125 mL
2 Tbsp	lemon juice	30 mL
1 Tbsp	minced garlic	15 mL
12	jumbo shrimp (21/25), head off, shell on, and deveined	12
1/8 tsp	freshly ground white pepper	0.5 mL
12	baguette slices cut 1/4 inch (6 mm) thick	12
1 Tbsp	extra virgin olive oil	15 mL
1 1/2 tsp	finely minced jalapeño pepper	7 mL

METHOD

To make the avocado butter, place three-quarters of the lime juice with the avocado, onion, salt and pepper, and chipotle and ancho peppers in a blender or food processor. Blend and taste. Add the basil and more lime juice if you like. Refrigerate, covered, if not using within the hour. Bring to room temperature before assembly.

For the shrimp, pour the vegetable oil into a dish large enough to hold all the shrimp in one layer. Mix the lemon juice and the garlic into the oil. Toss the shrimp in the oil until they are well coated. Marinate at room temperature for half to three-quarters of an hour.

Heat a cast iron skillet or grill until very hot. Cook the shrimp on both sides until they are bright pink, approximately 90 seconds per side. Cool and peel.

For the crostini, toast or grill the bread and then brush with a little olive oil. Spread the avocado butter thickly over each slice and top with a warm shrimp. Garnish with some jalapeño pepper.

We have all made or at least eaten the traditional bruschetta with tomatoes and garlic, but this is hardly any more work and the results are sublime. Try serving these with a light salad of mixed greens for a luncheon or a starter course. Makes 3 dozen.

TOMATO PRAWN BRUSCHETTA

INGREDIENTS

1 lb	medium-large prawns (36/40), shelled and deveined	500 g
1	lemon, zest only, cut in julienne strips	1
1 tsp	lemon juice	5 mL
2 Tbsp	capers	30 mL
3 Tbsp	minced fresh basil	45 mL
4	garlic cloves, minced	4
¼ cup	olive oil	60 mL
1½ cups	seeded and diced tomatoes (about 7 Romas)	375 mL
to taste	salt and black pepper	to taste
1	baguette or ficelle, sliced ½ inch (1 cm) thick and grilled	1

METHOD

Blanch the prawns in 10 cups (2.5 L) of boiling water until they are just cooked, approximately 2–4 minutes. Place in a bowl of ice cold water to stop the cooking. Drain. When they are cool, chop the prawns into ¼-inch (6 mm) pieces.

Mix together the lemon zest, lemon juice, capers, basil, garlic, olive oil, and tomatoes. Season with salt and pepper. Mix in the prawns. Spoon 1–2 Tbsp (15–30 mL) of the topping on each slice of grilled baguette. Serve immediately.

We enjoyed these as we packed like sardines into a tapas bar in San Sebastián. The tarts were easy to pop into our mouths as we were jostled by the crowds fueling up before an important soccer match. Makes 12 tarts.

SHRIMP & MUSHROOM TARTS

INGREDIENTS

1 Tbsp	extra virgin olive oil	15 mL
⅓ cup	finely minced onion	75 mL
2 Tbsp	finely minced green pepper	30 mL
2	garlic cloves, minced	2
1 cup	minced button mushrooms	250 mL
½ cup	plain tomato sauce	125 mL
2 Tbsp	brandy	30 mL
¼ cup	whipping cream (35%)	60 mL
1 cup	minced, cooked baby shrimp	250 mL
to taste	coarse salt and ground black pepper	to taste
12	2-inch (5 cm) frozen tart shells, baked	12
to taste	parsley and grated Parmesan	to taste

METHOD

In a sauté pan over medium-high heat, add the oil, onion, and pepper. Sauté for 5 minutes until the onion is tender. Add the garlic and mushrooms and sauté until the mushrooms are soft and the pan is dry. Add the tomato sauce, brandy, and cream and cook 5 minutes to reduce. Add shrimp, warm through, and season to taste. Spoon into the baked tart shells and garnish with chopped parsley and Parmesan cheese. Serve warm.

This is the typical shrimp cocktail that used to be on every menu. Did we ever really get tired of it? Use tall martini glasses for a fun presentation. *Serves 16.*

SPICY SHRIMP COCKTAIL

INGREDIENTS

4 cups	water	1 L
2	small onions	2
4	garlic cloves, crushed	4
2	jalapeño peppers, cut in half	2
2 lb	jumbo shrimp (21/25), peeled and deveined	1 kg
1 cup	ketchup	250 mL
¼ cup	horseradish	60 mL
3 Tbsp	fresh lime juice	45 mL
2	squirts Tabasco sauce	2
2	squirts Worcestershire sauce	2
8 cups	shredded iceberg lettuce	2 L
4	lemons, quartered	4

METHOD

In a saucepan, bring the 4 cups (1 L) water to a boil with the onions, garlic, and jalapeño. Add the shrimp, turn off the heat, and let sit 6 minutes. Remove the shrimp and cool in ice water. Drain and chill completely.

To make the cocktail sauce, blend the ketchup with the horseradish, lime juice, Tabasco, and Worcestershire. This sauce can be made several days ahead of time and kept in the refrigerator.

To serve, place the shredded lettuce in a martini glass, top with the sauce, and hang 3 shrimp on the rim. Garnish each with a wedge of lemon.

This is a recipe given to me by LA chef Michael Roberts many years ago during a summer I did some on-air work on KUSC. He signed my copy of his cookbook: "Eating well is the best revenge," and I've been resoundingly vengeful ever since, especially with this excellent party appetizer. If you're doubling quantities, don't double the amount of sesame oil. Serves 4.

FIERY PRAWNS
IN ORANGE JUICE

INGREDIENTS

1	orange, grated zest of	1
1 cup	fresh orange juice, without pulp	250 mL
2 Tbsp	fresh lemon juice	30 mL
1 or 2	cinnamon sticks, broken into pieces	1 or 2
½ tsp	cayenne (more or less)	2 mL
1 tsp	salt	5 mL
1 tsp	dark sesame oil (more or less)	5 mL
20	jumbo prawns (21/25), peeled and deveined with tails on	20
to garnish	tomato slices, ripe avocado wedges, chopped parsley	to garnish

METHOD

Combine the orange zest, orange juice, lemon juice, cinnamon sticks, cayenne, salt, and sesame oil in a medium saucepan over high heat. Bring to the boil, cover, and cook 2 minutes.

Put the prawns in a glass bowl and pour the boiling marinade over. Cover and let cool to room temperature. Take out the cinnamon sticks if you want only a hint of that flavor, otherwise leave them in. Refrigerate overnight.

Just before serving, arrange the tomatoes and avocados on a platter, put the prawns artfully on or around, and spoon cold marinade over everything. Sprinkle with parsley. The tails are your pick-up utensils.

This hands-on summer app is simple and delicious—perfect for serving to friends who drop by with a bottle of Tijuana's finest and a bag of fresh limes. Prepare it on the side burner of your gas grill and flambé if you dare! Makes 4–6 servings.

LIME TEQUILA PEEL-&-EAT SHRIMP

INGREDIENTS

1 lb	extra-jumbo shrimp (16/20), deveined, shell on	500 g
3 Tbsp	tequila	45 mL
2	garlic cloves, minced	2
2 Tbsp	fresh lime juice	30 mL
2 tsp	lime zest	10 mL
¼ tsp	hot pepper flakes	1 mL
3 Tbsp	butter	45 mL

METHOD

Combine the shrimp, tequila, garlic, lime juice, lime zest, and pepper flakes in a medium bowl. Cover and refrigerate for 15–30 minutes. Melt the butter in a large skillet over medium-high heat. Add the shrimp and cook until firm and bright pink, about 2–3 minutes. Transfer to a serving dish and enjoy.

This is an excellent party dish. You can lay out all of the ingredients and instruct your guests how to roll their own! It takes a bit of practice to roll these. What you are aiming for is an even, tight roll. Make sure that all of the ingredients are well tucked into the lettuce and somen noodles, or errant pieces of cucumber will poke through the rice paper. Makes 24 rolls.

SHRIMP SALAD ROLLS

INGREDIENTS

24	8-inch (20 cm) rice papers	24
12	large leaves of leaf lettuce, cut in half lengthwise	12
¼ lb	somen noodles, cooked and cooled	125 g
3 cups	cooked baby shrimp, fresh, or if frozen, thawed and well drained	750 mL
1 cup	packed mint leaves	250 mL
1	small bunch cilantro, coarse stems removed	1
½	English cucumber, seeded and coarsely julienned	½
12	green onions, split in half lengthwise and cut into 1-inch (2.5 cm) pieces	12
1	recipe Sweet and Sour Dipping Sauce (see recipe next page)	1
¼ cup	finely chopped roasted peanuts	60 mL

METHOD

Have a large bowl of hot water handy to dip the rice papers into. Take a sheet of rice paper and quickly dip it into the hot water and place it on a flat surface. Dip as many papers as you have room for.

When the papers have become pliable, place the filling ingredients close to the bottom of the papers in this order: lettuce, then a small pile of somen noodles, shrimp, a few mint leaves and a few cilantro sprigs, the cucumber, and some green onion.

Smear a bit of the somen noodles at the top of the paper. This will help the roll stick together. Pick up the bottom edge and fold it over the filling. Fold the sides over the filling. Roll from the bottom, gently but firmly. Continue with the remaining rice papers and filling. Place the dipping sauce in bowls and sprinkle with peanuts. Serve immediately with the dipping sauce.

Recipe continues on page 116 . . .

INGREDIENTS — continued

Sweet and Sour Dipping Sauce
Makes 3 cups (750 mL).

1½ cups	granulated sugar	375 mL
2 cups	water	500 mL
4	garlic cloves, peeled and sliced	4
½	red bell pepper, green stem only removed	½
3 Tbsp	fish sauce	45 mL
5 Tbsp	fresh lime juice	75 mL
1 tsp	sea salt	5 mL
1 Tbsp	hot chili paste or to taste	15 mL

METHOD — continued

Place the sugar and water in a saucepan and bring to a boil. Boil for 10 minutes, remove from the heat and cool.

Place ½ cup (125 mL) of the sugar syrup and the remaining ingredients in the bowl of a food processor or blender and blend until the pepper and garlic are puréed. The seeds will remain whole. Add the remaining sugar syrup and pulse briefly to combine. This sauce keeps almost forever, covered and refrigerated.

To add another dimension of flavor, you can use lemongrass cut into 4-inch (10 cm) lengths instead of the bamboo skewers. Makes 12 lollipops.

SHRIMP LOLLIPOPS

INGREDIENTS

1 cup	raw shrimp, peeled and deveined	250 mL
1	shallot, peeled and finely chopped	1
½	jalapeño pepper, seeded and finely minced	½
½	sweet pepper, seeded and finely chopped	½
1 Tbsp	finely chopped cilantro	15 mL
pinch	cayenne pepper	pinch
1 Tbsp	sesame seeds, lightly toasted	15 mL
2 cups	vegetable oil, for deep frying	500 mL
½ cup	all-purpose flour	125 mL
2	eggs, slightly beaten	2
1 cup	bread crumbs	250 mL
to taste	kosher salt and white pepper	to taste

METHOD

Purée the shrimp in a food processor until smooth. Transfer the shrimp purée to a stainless steel bowl. Add the shallot, jalapeño, sweet pepper, cilantro, cayenne, and sesame seeds and combine thoroughly. Refrigerate for 3 hours.

Remove the shrimp purée from the fridge and, using your hands, form 12 balls (each ball of shrimp mix should be the circumference of a nickel). Insert an 8-inch (20 cm) wooden skewer into each shrimp ball. Refrigerate.

Heat the deep-frying oil to 360°F (185°C).

Take the shrimp lollipops from the fridge and dip each one first into the flour, then the egg, and finally the bread crumbs. Make sure each lollipop is well coated with bread crumbs. Carefully lower each shrimp into the hot oil and fry until golden brown.

These make great pass-around hors d'oeuvres at cocktail parties. I don't think caterers could survive without a variation of these in their recipe repertoire. For a seafood mix, follow the same technique using sea scallops and crab fingers. If you're entertaining and want to get ahead, you can fry these shrimp ahead of time and keep them warm in a 200°F (95°C) oven. Serves 6.

COCONUT SHRIMP
WITH CITRUS DIPPING SAUCE

INGREDIENTS

¾ lb	raw shrimp, medium large to jumbo (21/40), peeled and deveined	375 g
½ cup	cornstarch	125 mL
¾ tsp	fine salt	4 mL
¼ tsp	ground black pepper	1 mL
3 cups	sweetened shredded coconut	750 mL
3	large egg whites	3
for frying	vegetable oil	for frying
2 Tbsp	fresh lime juice	30 mL
2 Tbsp	fresh orange juice	30 mL
¼ cup	honey	60 mL
1 tsp	freshly grated ginger	5 mL
1 tsp	Dijon mustard	5 mL
to taste	salt	to taste
to taste	hot sauce	to taste

METHOD

For the shrimp, run a paring knife down the back of each shrimp, to split open without cutting all the way through (this is "butterflying"). Toss the cornstarch, salt, and pepper together in one bowl and pour the coconut into another bowl. In a third bowl, whip the egg whites until frothy.

Pour enough vegetable oil into a deep pot or skillet to a depth of 2 inches (5 cm), and heat to 350°F (180°C), using a fryer or sugar thermometer to measure the temperature. Dredge each shrimp in the cornstarch, shake off the excess, then dip into the egg whites, again shaking off the excess, then press the shrimp into the coconut. Fry a few shrimp at a time until cooked through, 1–2 minutes. Drain the cooked shrimp on a paper towel.

To make the citrus dipping sauce, whisk together the lime juice, orange juice, honey, ginger, Dijon mustard, salt, and hot sauce and season to taste. Chill until ready to serve.

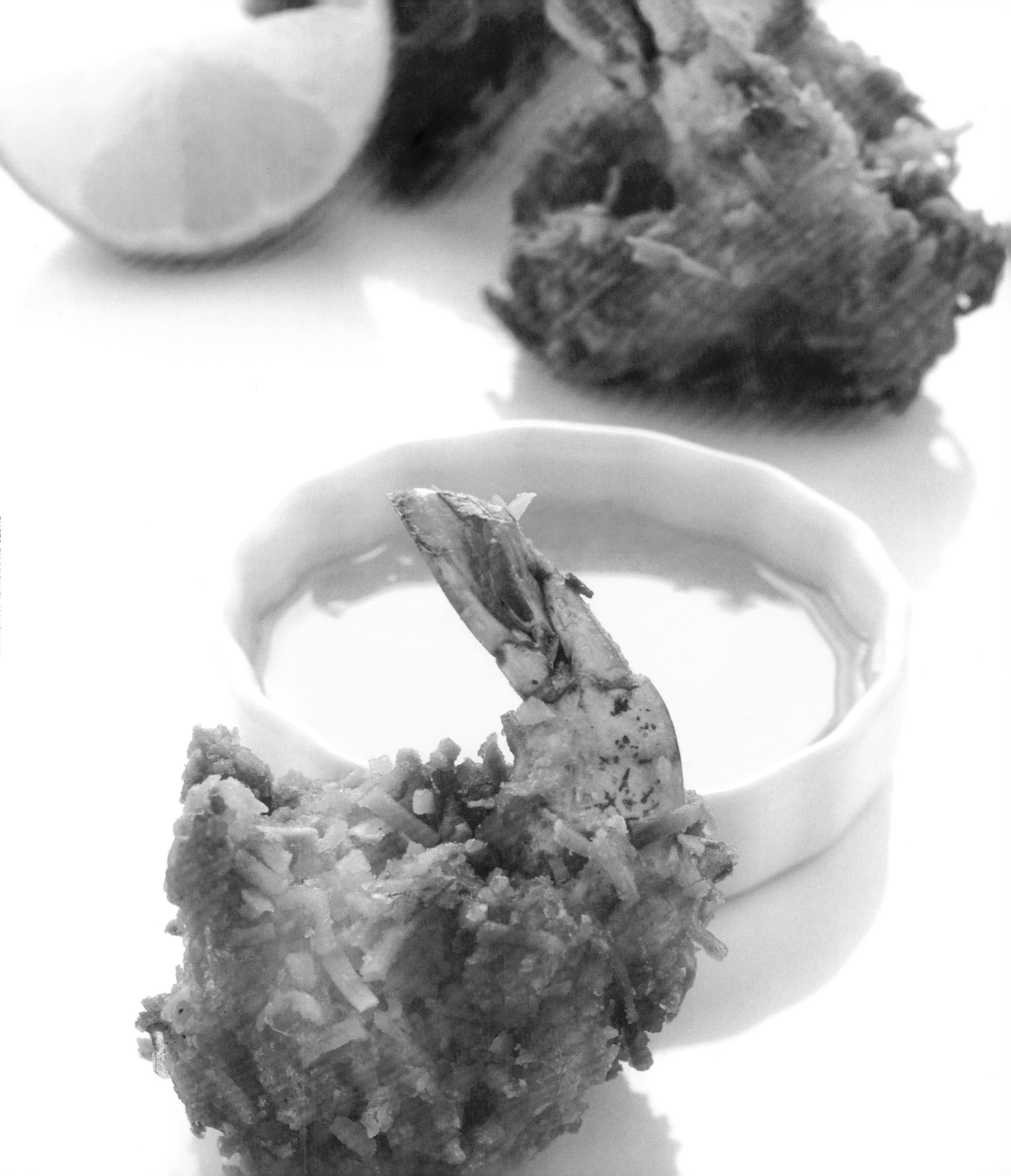

PHOTO BY MICHAEL MAHOVLICH

I was very fortunate to be invited on several occasions to be a guest chef with Crystal Cruises. This dish was featured on the menu and I was assured that never more than 30 percent of diners chose this menu. The first sitting began in normal fashion, but within 20 minutes we found ourselves doing second and third helpings. So whatever your thoughts are regarding numbers, double it. Makes 18 pieces.

PROSCIUTTO-WRAPPED PRAWNS
WITH BASIL DIPPING SAUCE

INGREDIENTS

2	large shallots, peeled	2
2 cups	firmly packed fresh basil leaves	500 mL
2–3	garlic cloves, peeled	2–3
3 Tbsp	pine nuts	45 mL
2 tsp	balsamic vinegar	10 mL
½ cup	extra virgin olive oil	125 mL
to taste	sea salt	to taste
to taste	Tellicherry pepper or black pepper	to taste
18	extra-jumbo (16/20) prawns, peeled and deveined with tail left on	18
9	thin slices of prosciutto, preferably Italian	9

METHOD

Lightly rub the shallots with olive oil. Place them in a garlic roaster or wrap in foil and bake at 325°F (160°C) for about 40 minutes, or until they are soft and golden in color.

Place the roasted shallots, basil, garlic, pine nuts, and vinegar in a blender or food processor and purée until the mixture is smooth, scraping down the sides of the bowl once or twice. With the motor running, slowly pour in the olive oil. The sauce will thicken slightly. Season with the sea salt and the Tellicherry pepper.

Dry the prawns thoroughly. Cut the prosciutto in half lengthwise and wrap one piece around the body of each prawn. Rub the wrapped prawn with a scant amount of olive oil. Heat a barbecue or grill to high. Cook the prawns until they are bright pink, turning only once. This should take about 3–4 minutes. Serve hot off the grill with the basil sauce.

When my first book, *Pacific Passions*, came out many people asked, "Are flaming prawns in it?" "Next book," I would say. From *Screamingly Good Food*, these are the flaming prawns, one of the most popular dishes at the Fish House in Stanley Park. Serves 4 as an appetizer, 2 as a main course.

FLAMING PRAWNS!

INGREDIENTS

1 Tbsp	extra virgin olive oil	15 mL
1 tsp	minced garlic	5 mL
24	jumbo prawns (21/25), peeled and deveined	24
½ cup	coarsely chopped roasted sweet red peppers	125 mL
½ cup	coarsely chopped, drained canned Italian plum tomatoes	125 mL
½ cup	crumbled feta cheese	125 mL
¼ cup	fresh basil leaves	60 mL
½ cup	fresh spinach leaves	125 mL
1 oz	ouzo, in a shot glass or small glass	30 mL
½	lemon, seeds removed	½

METHOD

In a large skillet, heat the olive oil over high heat. Add the garlic; when it sizzles, add the prawns and stir-fry until they turn pink. Add the roasted peppers and tomatoes and stir-fry until the prawns are cooked through.

While the prawns are cooking, heat a heavy, preferably cast iron, pan over high heat. Have a wooden board ready to place the pan on, and have the ouzo and lemon ready.

Add the feta and basil to the prawns and stir to combine. Transfer to one side of the second heated pan and place the pan on the board. Carry the board to the table and advise everyone to stay well back. Pour the ouzo into the empty side of the pan and ignite immediately with a long match. Squeeze the lemon over the prawns to douse the flames, and stir. If pyrotechnics are not your style, just add the ouzo to the prawns after they have finished cooking. This, however, lacks drama. Serve with pasta, rice, or bread to mop up the juices.

This salad is similar to a colorful coleslaw and it is often served in a hollowed-out red cabbage. It is an ideal choice for people wanting a very low-fat dressing, as it is completely oil free. You could substitute cooked diced chicken for the shrimp. Serves 4.

NORTHERN THAI SHRIMP SALAD

INGREDIENTS

5 Tbsp	lime juice	75 mL
¼ cup	fish sauce	60 mL
½ tsp	cayenne powder	2 mL
½ cup	minced onion	125 mL
1 Tbsp	minced fresh ginger	15 mL
½ cup	water or stock	125 mL
¼ cup	chopped green onion	60 mL
2 Tbsp	coarsely chopped mint leaves	30 mL
¼ cup	coarsely chopped cilantro leaves	60 mL
1 lb	cooked baby shrimp	500 g
½ cup	finely sliced red cabbage	125 mL
½ cup	finely sliced green cabbage	125 mL
1 cup	grated carrot	250 mL
1 cup	finely sliced cucumber	250 mL
1 cup	finely sliced green bell pepper	250 mL
4	large lettuce leaves, sliced	4

METHOD

To make the dressing, combine the lime juice, fish sauce, cayenne powder, minced onion, ginger, and water or stock in a saucepan. Bring to a boil, then lower the heat to a simmer and cook for about 5 minutes. Remove from the heat and let cool. The dressing can be refrigerated for up to 2 days.

Toss the remaining ingredients, except for the sliced lettuce, along with the dressing just before serving. Place on a bed of the sliced lettuce.

This is another salad that can be used as a main course. Buy the freshest, best-quality shrimp. The vinaigrette adds texture and bright flavors; the fennel, a wonderful crunch. Serves 4.

FRISÉE

WITH HAND-PEELED SHRIMP
& CILANTRO VINAIGRETTE

INGREDIENTS

1	bulb fennel	1
2	small heads of frisée or curly endive	2
¼	red bell pepper, finely diced	¼
¼	yellow bell pepper, finely diced	¼
1 Tbsp	finely diced red onion	15 mL
½	Granny Smith apple, peeled and finely diced	½
2 Tbsp	fresh lemon juice	30 mL
½ cup	rice vinegar	125 mL
1 Tbsp	chopped cilantro	15 mL
½ tsp	salt	2 mL
½ tsp	freshly ground black pepper	2 mL
½ cup	olive oil	125 mL
8 oz	fresh hand-peeled shrimp, or cooked baby shrimp	225 g

METHOD

Cut the fennel bulb in half lengthwise, remove the core, and slice as thinly as possible. Submerge in ice water for 1–1½ hours before serving. This will crisp and curl the fennel.

Pull the frisée apart, discarding the outer leaves and stem. Soak the leaves in cold water and pat dry.

To make the vinaigrette, combine the diced peppers, onion, and apple. Stir in the lemon juice. In a separate small bowl whisk together the rice vinegar, cilantro, and salt and pepper. Slowly whisk in the olive oil. Combine with the other ingredients. Make the vinaigrette at least 1 hour before serving. Serve at room temperature.

Arrange the frisée in the centers of 4 salad plates. Arrange 2 oz (50 g) of shrimp on the endive. Drizzle the vinaigrette over the salad and onto the plate. Spoon some of the apples and peppers out of the vinaigrette and place in 1 or 2 small stacks on each plate. Place a small stack of sliced fennel atop each salad.

Without the shrimp, this twist on the traditional panzanella salad works well with grilled steak, fish, or chicken. Include the shrimp and it becomes a perfect summer or early fall meal. Vary the proportions of peppers, green onions, croutons, and tomatoes to suit your taste. Serves 4 generously.

SUMMER BREAD SALAD
WITH GRILLED LEMON-PEPPER SHRIMP

INGREDIENTS

10	jumbo shrimp (21/25), marinated (see method)	10
¾	of a yellow pepper, cut lengthwise in 1-inch (2.5 cm) strips, brushed with oil and grilled or roasted	¾
½	of a red pepper, cut lengthwise in 1-inch (2.5 cm) strips, brushed with oil and grilled or roasted	½
15	green onions, white and pale green part only, brushed with oil and grilled or roasted	15
20	croutons	20
25	cherry tomatoes, cut in half	25
3 Tbsp	red wine vinegar	45 mL
½ tsp	minced garlic	2 mL
5 Tbsp	olive oil	75 mL
to taste	salt and freshly ground black pepper	to taste
8–10	large basil leaves, roughly torn	8–10

METHOD

Devein the shrimp but leave them in the shell. Marinate in 3 parts olive oil to 1 part lemon juice, black pepper, and some minced garlic for 20 minutes to an hour before grilling. Grill the shrimp and let cool for 10 minutes. Shell and slice lengthwise. If possible, add them to the salad while they are still slightly warm.

To make the salad, put the peppers, onions, croutons, tomatoes, and shrimp in a large serving bowl. To make the dressing, combine the vinegar and the minced garlic. Slowly whisk in the oil. Add salt and pepper. Adjust the vinegar and oil mixture to taste. It should be slightly on the tart side.

Pour three-quarters of the vinaigrette over the salad, add more if needed, and let marinate at room temperature for 15–20 minutes. Add the torn basil just before serving and toss again.

Like traditional paella, this salad cannot be made in small quantities. Make a pitcher of sangria and invite some friends over for a summer lunch. You could add mussels and/or scallops to this dish for a salad really packed with seafood. Serves 8–10.

SUMMER PAELLA SALAD

INGREDIENTS

⅓ cup	olive oil	75 mL
4 tsp	lemon juice	20 mL
1 Tbsp	chopped fresh oregano	15 mL
1 Tbsp	chopped fresh basil	15 mL
1 tsp	freshly ground black pepper	5 mL
2 Tbsp	minced garlic	30 mL
6	boneless skinless chicken breasts	6
1 lb	jumbo prawns (21/25), peeled with the tails left on	500 g
1½ cups	basmati rice	375 mL
2½ cups	water	625 mL
¼ tsp	saffron	1 mL
½	yellow bell pepper, julienned	½
½	red bell pepper, julienned	½
¾ cup	thinly sliced green onion	175 mL
1 cup	peeled, diced tomatoes	250 mL
½ cup	pitted green olives, cut into quarters	125 mL
to taste	salt and black pepper	to taste

Vinaigrette

¾ cup	extra virgin olive oil	175 mL
1 Tbsp	finely minced garlic	15 mL
1 Tbsp	fresh oregano	15 mL
1 Tbsp	fresh basil	15 mL
½ tsp	turmeric	2 mL
½ tsp	paprika	2 mL
3 Tbsp	lemon juice	45 mL
to taste	salt and black pepper	to taste

METHOD

Mix the olive oil, lemon juice, oregano, basil, pepper, and garlic in a shallow dish. Coat the chicken with this mixture and marinate not more than 2 hours. Broil or grill the chicken breasts 4–5 minutes per side. Let cool and slice into 2- x ½-inch (5 x 1 cm) pieces. Set aside.

Bring a medium saucepan of water to a boil. Add the prawns and blanch for 1 minute, or just until the prawns turn opaque. Drain and rinse with cold water. Set aside.

Wash the basmati rice, drain, and place in a medium saucepan with the water and saffron. Bring to a boil, then lower the heat to a slow simmer. Cover and cook 12–15 minutes, until all the water is absorbed.

While the rice is cooking make the vinaigrette by heating ¾ cup (175 mL) olive oil in a small saucepan. Add 1 Tbsp (15 mL) of garlic and sauté for 1 minute.

Remove from the heat and mix in the oregano, basil, turmeric, paprika, lemon juice, and salt and pepper.

Once the rice is cooked and still warm, toss with the vinaigrette. Add the peppers, green onions, tomatoes, and olives. Toss well and add the chicken and prawns. Season to taste and serve.

The two best ways to enjoy fennel are braised very slowly in the oven with a few spices, or raw and marinated. This recipe brings a sunshine smile to my face; it's a perfectly intense and crisp summer dish. Serves 6.

ORANGE-FLAVORED FENNEL SALAD & PRAWNS

INGREDIENTS

2	large fennel bulbs	2
to taste	salt and pepper	to taste
2 Tbsp	fresh lemon juice	30 mL
¼ cup	freshly squeezed orange juice	60 mL
½ cup	virgin olive oil	125 mL
12	extra-jumbo prawns (16/20)	12
3 Tbsp	virgin olive oil	45 mL
4–5	dill sprigs	4–5

METHOD

Two hours before serving the salad, cut the fennel bulbs in half lengthwise and remove the core. Thinly slice the halves lengthwise. Place the slices in a large salad bowl and season with salt and pepper. Add the lemon juice, orange juice, and the ½ cup (125 mL) oil. Stir well and let marinate in the refrigerator for at least 1 hour.

Just before serving the salad, sauté the prawns in the remaining 3 Tbsp (45 mL) oil on high heat. Place on the cold marinated salad. Garnish with dill.

For a perfect romantic dinner, all you really need is Shrimp in Love, a loaf of crusty bread, your favorite wine—and a date! Although this makes an excellent appetizer, it is also great when served with rice or pasta as a main course. It's the best way to eat shrimp. Serves 4.

SHRIMP IN LOVE

INGREDIENTS

20	jumbo shrimp (21/25), peeled, deveined, and butterflied	20
2 Tbsp	olive oil	30 mL
2	garlic cloves, minced	2
1 Tbsp	minced shallot or onion	15 mL
½ cup	brandy	125 mL
1 cup	tomato sauce	250 mL
1 cup	whipping cream (35%)	250 mL
to taste	salt and white pepper	to taste
½ cup	finely sliced green onions or scallions	125 mL
1 Tbsp	cold unsalted butter	15 mL

METHOD

In a large skillet on medium heat, sauté the shrimp quickly (about 2 minutes) in the olive oil to medium-rare and remove from the pan, leaving the oil behind. Using the same pan, sweat the garlic and shallots to a light brown. Deglaze with the brandy, then add the tomato sauce and cream. Simmer 3 minutes, and add salt and pepper. Return the shrimp to the pan. Add the green onions or scallions and whisk in the cold butter.

Piggyback 5 shrimp over each other on each of the plates and cover with the sauce. That's why they are in love!

TIP

Make sure you remove the shrimp after the first 2 minutes to ensure they don't overcook and become rubbery. Make the sauce, then fold the shrimp back into the hot sauce and serve immediately.

Vanilla and shellfish together may seem like an unlikely marriage of flavors, but it's a match made in heaven. Pile these on a platter with a small bowl for the discarded tails. If you want a main course serving suggestion, add some whipping cream to the pan to make the dish more "saucy," reduce to a thick consistency, and serve over rice. Serves 6–8 as an appetizer, 4 as a main course.

SHRIMP

IN VANILLA-INFUSED BUTTER

INGREDIENTS

1 Tbsp	olive oil	15 mL
¼ cup	butter	60 mL
1	vanilla pod, cut lengthwise, seeds scraped out and reserved	1
24	jumbo shrimp (21/25), peeled and with the tails left on	24

METHOD

Heat the oil in a sauté pan over medium heat and add the butter. Reduce the heat to low, add the vanilla (both seeds and pods), and heat gently until fragrant, about 5 minutes. Be sure not to use too high a heat because the vanilla may scorch and have an unpleasant flavor. Remove the vanilla pods and discard. Remove half of the butter and reserve.

Turn the heat up to medium-high and place 10 shrimp in the pan in a single layer. Cook on one side for about 2 minutes, or until they have started to change color slightly. Flip and cook for another minute, or just until the shrimp have lost their translucent look. Do not overcook the shrimp; they become tough and unappetizing. Add more of the butter mixture to the pan, if needed, and repeat with the next 10 shrimp.

San Sebastián is one of my favorite Spanish towns—loaded with great restaurants and tapas bars. This is where you'll find shrimp like this, piled on the bar, to enjoy with a glass of wine or a crisp, fino sherry. A real tapas bar specialty. Serves 4.

GRILLED PAPRIKA SHRIMP
WITH GARLIC SAUCE

INGREDIENTS

2	garlic cloves, minced	2
¼ cup	extra virgin olive oil	60 mL
½ cup	mayonnaise	125 mL
2 Tbsp	extra virgin olive oil	30 mL
1 tsp	Dijon mustard	5 mL
2	garlic cloves, minced	2
to taste	salt and freshly ground black pepper	to taste
1 tsp	sherry vinegar or freshly squeezed lemon juice	5 mL
1 tsp	hot Spanish paprika	5 mL
1 lb	jumbo shrimp (21/25), peeled and deveined, tails on	500 g
to taste	fresh Italian parsley, chopped	to taste

METHOD

Combine the garlic and ¼ cup (60 mL) olive oil in a bowl and set aside for 30 minutes to infuse.

To make the garlic sauce, whisk together the mayonnaise, 2 Tbsp (30 mL) olive oil, Dijon mustard, and minced garlic. Season with salt and pepper and refrigerate.

Remove the garlic-infused olive oil from the refrigerator and whisk in the vinegar and paprika. Add the shrimp, stirring to coat well.

Skewer each shrimp on parallel bamboo skewers, running the skewers through both the head and tail end of the shrimp (this helps the shrimp to lie flat on the grill). Grill the shrimp over medium-high heat for 1 minute per side or just until they turn pink and opaque.

Pull the shrimp from the skewers, toss with fresh parsley, and serve with the garlic sauce for dipping.

When researching this recipe I asked several Indian cooks for advice and each one gave me a different answer. What was common was the use of lots of butter and whipping cream. Butter curry is usually prepared with tandoori baked chicken, which can result in a rather lengthy recipe. Since prawns cook so quickly, they make a great substitution. Serves 4.

INDIAN BUTTER PRAWNS

INGREDIENTS

⅓ cup	plain yogurt	75 mL
½ tsp	fine sea salt	2 mL
28	jumbo prawns (21/25), peeled and deveined	28
20	whole almonds, toasted	20
2	garlic cloves	2
2 Tbsp	minced fresh ginger	30 mL
1 tsp	curry powder	5 mL
½ tsp	garam masala	2 mL
¼ tsp	chili powder	1 mL
2	green cardamom pods, ground	2
⅓ cup	unsalted butter	75 mL
5 Tbsp	tomato paste	75 mL
1 cup	chicken or vegetable stock	250 mL
1 tsp	honey	5 mL
⅓ cup	whipping cream (35%)	75 mL
⅓ cup	chopped fresh cilantro leaves	75 mL
to taste	salt and freshly ground black pepper	to taste

METHOD

In a medium bowl, combine the yogurt and salt. Fold in the prawns and set aside while preparing the sauce.

Place the almonds, garlic, ginger, curry powder, garam masala, chili powder, and cardamom in the bowl of a food processor. Use the steel knife attachment to blend the ingredients together.

In a large saucepan, melt the butter over medium heat. Add the almond and spice mix; cook, stirring often, for 3 minutes. Stir in the tomato paste and cook for another minute. Add the stock and honey and bring to a boil. Reduce the heat and simmer for 10 minutes. Pass the sauce through a fine mesh sieve, pressing down to extract all the liquid. Return to the saucepan.

Increase the heat to medium and stir in the prawns and cream. Cook about 3–5 minutes. Stir in the cilantro and seasonwith salt and pepper. Transfer the prawns and sauce to a warm dish and serve with steamed basmati rice or hot Indian bread.

Harissa is a very spicy condiment with its roots in Moroccan cuisine. If spice does not light up your life, use a scant teaspoon. Preserved lemon is also a common ingredient in Moroccan cooking. When using preserved lemons, discard the pulp and use only the rind. Both harissa and preserved lemon add a flavor dimension that is like no other. Try it, you'll love it! Serves 8 as an appetizer, 4 as a main course.

HARISSA PRAWNS

INGREDIENTS

2 Tbsp	olive oil	30 mL
2	large shallots, minced	2
2	garlic cloves, minced	2
1-inch piece	fresh ginger, peeled and minced	2.5 cm piece
2 tsp	anchovy paste	10 mL
1 Tbsp	smoked paprika	15 mL
2 Tbsp	harissa sauce	30 mL
2	whole tomatoes, peeled, seeded, and chopped	2
¼ cup	white wine	60 mL
to taste	sea salt	to taste
2 Tbsp	preserved lemon, chopped or	30 mL
2 tsp	freshly grated lemon rind	10 mL
24	jumbo prawns (21/25)	24

METHOD

Heat the olive oil in a medium sauté pan. Add the shallots, garlic, ginger, and anchovy paste, sautéing until fragrant and soft but not brown. Add the paprika, harissa, tomatoes, white wine, sea salt, and preserved lemon or fresh lemon rind. Continue to simmer until the sauce thickens. Taste for seasoning and let cool.

Peel the prawns, leaving the tail intact. When the sauce is cool, rub it over the prawns on all sides to coat well. Heat your grill or skillet to high heat and brush with a little oil. Add the prawns in a single layer, turning only once. As soon as they turn pink, remove from the pan, skewer with a fancy bamboo pick, and serve warm or at room temperature.

Gari, the sweet shaved ginger served with sushi, flatters prawns with its color and flavor. A pastel pink color means the ginger has been tinted. Natural gari is a honey color with only a hint of pink. Larger grocery stores now sell it chilled in jars and vacuum packs, or visit your local Japanese restaurant to buy a small amount. For a little heat, add a seeded and slivered jalapeño pepper to the presentation. Serves 4.

PRAWNS

WITH PINK GINGER & LIME SAUCE

INGREDIENTS

2 Tbsp	finely minced shallots	30 mL
1	garlic clove, finely minced	1
4 Tbsp	gari with juice	60 mL
1	lime, zest and juice of	1
2 Tbsp	mirin (sweet rice wine)	30 mL
6 Tbsp	chilled unsalted butter, cut into ½-inch (1 cm) cubes	90 mL
¼ tsp	salt	1 mL
1 Tbsp	oil or butter	15 mL
16–20	jumbo prawns (21/25), peeled and deveined	16–20
to garnish	cilantro leaves or chive sprigs	to garnish

METHOD

In a nonreactive saucepan, combine the shallot and garlic. Drain the ginger, reserving 2 Tbsp (30 mL) of the liquid. Finely mince the ginger and set aside. Combine the drained liquid from the ginger with the lime juice and mirin, which should equal ½ cup (125 mL) altogether. Add this to the saucepan. Boil the mixture gently to reduce the liquid by two-thirds. It will look like marmalade.

Over low heat, whisk in 2 pieces of butter. The sauce will look creamy white. Continue to whisk in the butter, piece by piece. Season with salt. Add the ginger and remove from the heat.

Heat the 1 Tbsp (15 mL) oil or butter in a skillet. Sear the prawns until they're opaque and pink. Serve the prawns with the sauce lightly spooned overtop and garnish with the lime zest and cilantro or chives.

This dish was inspired by a customer who asked me if I had ever heard of shrimp with chocolate sauce. I thought of Mexican moles and ancient Spanish dishes that use sweet spices and cocoa in their sauces, did some research and some cooking, and this is what I came up with. Although a mortar and pestle works best to pound the almonds and garlic to a paste, you can also use a food processor or a blender. Serves 3–4.

PRAWNS IN COCOA SAUCE

INGREDIENTS

¾ lb	large prawns (31/35)	375 g
1 Tbsp	olive oil	15 mL
1	whole dried chili	1
¼ cup	finely diced onion	60 mL
1 cup	well-drained, canned plum tomatoes, puréed and sieved to remove seeds	250 mL
¼ cup	red wine	60 mL
1	whole clove	1
½ tsp	cocoa	2 mL
¼ tsp	salt	1 mL
large pinch	sugar	large pinch
large pinch	cinnamon	large pinch
10	whole skinless almonds, toasted	10
1	small garlic clove, peeled	1
2 tsp	chopped parsley	10 mL

METHOD

Peel the prawns, saving the shells. Place the shells in a pot and cover with 1½ cups (375 mL) water. Bring to a boil and simmer for 20 minutes. Strain and reserve ½ cup (125 mL) of the liquid; discard the shells.

Heat the olive oil in a large, nonstick skillet over medium-low heat. Add the chili pepper and fry until it turns dark brown. Add the onion and puréed tomatoes. Cook, stirring frequently, for about 5 minutes. Discard the chili pepper. Add the red wine, reserved shrimp stock, whole clove, cocoa, salt, sugar, and cinnamon. Simmer over low heat for 5 minutes.

With a mortar and pestle, pound the almonds to a paste. Add the garlic clove and pound to a paste. Add a few spoonfuls of the tomato sauce to help it along. Add the chopped parsley. Add the prawns to the tomato mixture and cook until cooked through, about 3–4 minutes. Stir in the almond paste and serve.

I love romescu sauce! Try it on fish, pork, or chicken. It also makes a good dip for tortilla chips. Serves 4.

SEARED PRAWNS
WITH ROMESCU SAUCE

INGREDIENTS

¼ cup	extra virgin olive oil	60 mL
½ cup	finely chopped onion	125 mL
4	garlic cloves, minced	4
1	roasted red pepper, chopped	1
2	ripe tomatoes, peeled, seeded, and chopped	2
½ tsp	dried chili flakes	2 mL
5 Tbsp	fish stock or clam nectar	75 mL
2 Tbsp	white wine	30 mL
10	toasted almonds	10
1 Tbsp	red wine vinegar	15 mL
to taste	sea salt and freshly ground pepper	to taste
24	jumbo prawns (21/25), peeled and deveined	24
3 Tbsp	extra virgin olive oil	45 mL
to serve	lemon wedges	to serve

METHOD

Heat 2 Tbsp (30 mL) of the olive oil in a medium-sized pot, add the onion and 3 of the garlic cloves, and cook until the onion is soft. Add the pepper, tomatoes, chili, fish stock or clam nectar, and wine. Cover and simmer on low heat for 30 minutes, until thickened.

Transfer to a blender or food processor and purée coarsely. Add the remaining 2 Tbsp (30 mL) of oil, almonds, vinegar, and the last garlic clove and process until smooth. Season to taste.

Heat a heavy skillet over high heat. Toss the prawns in the 3 Tbsp (45 mL) olive oil, then spread out in the skillet. Sear for about 2–3 minutes on each side, until pink and cooked through. Arrange on a serving platter with the lemon wedges, and the sauce in a small bowl.

This is a simple stir-fry to make in the spring, when fresh asparagus is available. You can buy peeled frozen raw shrimp. Just don't get the precooked kind. Serves 4.

SHRIMP

WITH ASPARAGUS & CASHEW NUTS

INGREDIENTS

2 Tbsp	canola oil	30 mL
1 lb	jumbo shrimp (21/25), peeled and deveined	500 g
¼ cup	oyster sauce	60 mL
1 tsp	fish sauce	5 mL
1 Tbsp	vinegar	15 mL
1 tsp	Asian chili paste	5 mL
12	stalks of asparagus, cut into 2-inch (5 cm) pieces	12
½	red bell pepper, slivered	½
1	small onion, slivered	1
1 tsp	cornstarch mixed with 1 tsp (5 mL) water	5 mL
¼ cup	toasted cashews	60 mL

METHOD

In a wok or a large sauté pan, heat 1 Tbsp (15 mL) of canola oil over medium-high heat. Add the shrimp and cook just until it turns pink. Remove from the pan.

In a small bowl, combine the oyster sauce, fish sauce, vinegar, and chili paste.

Add the remaining 1 Tbsp (15 mL) of canola oil to the hot pan and add the asparagus, red pepper, and onion. Stir-fry over medium-high heat for 5 minutes or until the vegetables are tender and begin to brown. Add the sauce mixture and cook for 1 minute. Add the cornstarch solution and stir until the sauce bubbles and thickens (add a splash of broth or water if it seems too thick).

Return the shrimp to the wok and toss to heat through. Stir in the cashews and serve immediately.

This pasta captures the essence of late summer. Tomatoes, prawns, and basil are at their best and the bocconcini is ripe on the vine. Ha! Serves 4 as a main course, 6 as an appetizer.

SEASHELL PASTA
WITH TOMATOES, BOCCONCINI, PRAWNS & BASIL

INGREDIENTS

1½ lb	ripe plum tomatoes	750 g
2	garlic cloves, cut in half and lightly crushed	2
⅓ cup	extra virgin olive oil	75 mL
¾ tsp	sea salt	4 mL
½ tsp	coarsely and freshly ground black pepper	2 mL
½ cup	loosely packed fresh basil leaves	125 mL
2	good quality bocconcini, or 1 cup (250 mL) cherry bocconcini	2
1 lb	jumbo prawns (21/25), peeled and deveined	500 g
1 lb	medium-sized seashell pasta	500 g

METHOD

Peel, seed, and dice the tomatoes, and set aside.

Skewer the garlic on a toothpick (this will make it easier to retrieve later) and add to the tomatoes. Mix in the olive oil, salt, and pepper. Tear the basil into small pieces. Add to the tomatoes and stir well. Let the whole mixture marinate for at least an hour, or up to 4 hours. Dice the bocconcini and reserve. If you are using cherry bocconcini leave them whole.

Cut the prawns into 3 pieces crosswise and refrigerate until ready to serve.

Bring a large pot of water to a boil. Salt liberally—it should taste like seawater—and add the pasta. Cook until tender but firm to the bite. Drain and return to the pot over medium heat. Remove the garlic from the tomatoes. Add the prawns and the tomato sauce to the pasta. Stir gently until the prawn pieces are cooked through and the bocconcini starts to melt. Serve immediately in warm bowls.

This cooking-class favorite is great way of using our local hand-peeled shrimp. Its spicy sweet-sour flavor has universal appeal. Many people have confessed to making extra so they can eat it cold out of the fridge the next day! Serves 4.

SHRIMP PAD THAI

INGREDIENTS

½ lb	dried rice noodles, no wider than ¼ inch (6 mm)	250 g
2 Tbsp	oyster sauce	30 mL
½ cup	ketchup	125 mL
1 Tbsp	molasses	15 mL
2 Tbsp	sugar	30 mL
2 Tbsp	fish sauce	30 mL
¼ cup	water	60 mL
1 tsp	dried chili flakes	5 mL
¼ cup	vegetable oil	60 mL
6	garlic cloves, minced	6
2	eggs	2
1½ cups	cooked baby shrimp	375 mL
2 cups	bean sprouts	500 mL
2 cups	Chinese chives or green onions, cut into 1-inch (2.5 cm) lengths	500 mL
2 Tbsp	chopped roasted peanuts	30 mL
to garnish	cilantro sprigs	to garnish

METHOD

Place the rice noodles in a bowl and cover with warm water for 30 minutes. Combine the oyster sauce, ketchup, molasses, sugar, fish sauce, water, and chili flakes in a small bowl and set aside.

Heat the vegetable oil in a wok or large skillet over high heat. Stir-fry the garlic until golden. Add the eggs and scramble until dry. Drain the noodles and add them to the pan. Stir-fry until the noodles soften, become shiny, and start sticking together in a mass. This is crucial to the texture of the finished dish. Add the shrimp, bean sprouts, chives or green onions, and the sauce. Cook until the sauce is absorbed. Turn out onto a platter and garnish with peanuts and cilantro.

Fried rice plays a big role in Thai families, where it is served frequently as a one-dish meal. It is an adaptable and practical dish that is usually based on leftovers, and with a little imagination and a few basic techniques, an infinite variety is possible. If you would like more prawns, double the amount. Serves 4.

PRAWN & BASIL FRIED RICE

INGREDIENTS

12	medium prawns (41/50), peeled	12
¼ cup	vegetable oil	60 mL
2 tsp	chopped garlic	10 mL
1 tsp	diced fresh chilies	5 mL
1 tsp	sugar	5 mL
2 tsp	dark soy sauce	10 mL
1 Tbsp	fish sauce	15 mL
½ cup	sliced Thai basil leaves	125 mL
2 cups	cooked and cooled jasmine rice	500 mL
1	long English cucumber, thinly sliced	1

METHOD

Slice the prawns in half, lengthwise. Heat the oil in a wok over high heat and fry the garlic and chili until the garlic is fragrant, less than a minute.

Add the prawn halves and stir-fry for 15 seconds over high heat. Add the sugar, soy sauce, and fish sauce. Stir thoroughly and add the basil leaves. Add the rice and stir-fry on high heat until it's hot. Serve on a platter surrounded by cucumber slices.

Starches go very well with curry. This is like having fries with gravy—and since this recipe is from a seafood restaurant, we add some shrimp. Serves 4.

YAM FRIES

WITH CURRIED SHRIMP

INGREDIENTS

2 Tbsp	oil or butter	30 mL
1 Tbsp	minced onion	15 mL
½ tsp	minced garlic	2 mL
½ tsp	minced fresh ginger	2 mL
½ tsp	salt	2 mL
½ tsp	curry powder	2 mL
pinch	ground cumin, coriander, garam masala, cinnamon, pepper, and turmeric	pinch
1 Tbsp	chopped seeded tomato	15 mL
1 Tbsp	chopped green onion	15 mL
½ cup	vegetable stock	125 mL
6 oz	cooked baby shrimp	175 g
2 lb	yams	1 kg
4 cups	vegetable oil	1 L
pinch	salt and black pepper	pinch

METHOD

Heat the 2 Tbsp (30 mL) oil or butter in a sauté pan over medium heat. Add the onion, garlic, ginger, salt, curry powder, and ground spices and cook for 1 minute. Add the tomato, green onion, cilantro, and stock. Cook for 3–5 minutes, until the sauce is thick. Stir in the shrimp. Keep warm.

Cut the yams into ¼- x 4-inch (0.5 x 10 cm) batons. Heat the oil in a deep, heavy pot to 350°F (180°C). Add the yams and cook for 3–5 minutes. I like the yams a little underdone and golden brown. Remove and place on a paper towel to drain. Dust with salt and pepper. Place the fries in a bowl and top with the curried shrimp.

These sweet and spicy kabobs are easy to prepare and are perfect for summer entertaining on the patio.
Serves 4.

THAI SHRIMP &
MANGO KABOBS

INGREDIENTS

4	large bamboo skewers	4
¼ cup	water	60 mL
¼ cup	rice vinegar	60 mL
2 Tbsp	granulated sugar	30 mL
¼ cup	Alizé Gold Passion liqueur	60 mL
2 Tbsp	fresh lime juice	30 mL
1	garlic clove, minced	1
½ tsp	hot pepper flakes	2 mL
12	colossal shrimp (U/15), peeled and deveined	12
2	semiripe mangoes, peeled and each cut into 8 bite-sized pieces	2

METHOD

Soak the skewers in warm water for 30 minutes to prevent scorching on the grill.

Heat the water, vinegar, and sugar in a small saucepan over medium heat until the sugar dissolves. Remove from the heat and let cool. Add the liqueur, lime juice, garlic, and pepper flakes.

Assemble 3 shrimp and 4 mango pieces on each skewer, alternating between fruit and shrimp. Arrange in a single layer in a baking dish and pour the marinade over. Refrigerate for 30 minutes, turning once.

Preheat the grill to medium-high heat.

Place the kabobs on the grill, close the lid, and cook for 3 minutes per side or until the shrimp are bright pink and firm. Be careful not to overcook.

I first made this dish when I was the executive chef at Taboo Restaurant in Toronto in the early 1990s. I was then asked to make an appearance live on CTV's *Eye on Toronto* show. During the rush of the live demonstration, I forgot a tray of shrimp in the oven and remembered only as I was driving home. I was never invited back! Serves 6.

LEMONGRASS SHRIMP SKEWERS

INGREDIENTS

1 Tbsp	honey	15 mL
2 Tbsp	olive oil	30 mL
2 tsp	sesame oil	10 mL
4	garlic cloves, crushed and finely chopped	4
1 Tbsp	finely chopped fresh ginger	15 mL
2	jalapeño peppers, finely chopped	2
2	limes, juice and zest of	2
1 Tbsp	finely chopped coriander	15 mL
4 Tbsp	rice wine vinegar	60 mL
2 Tbsp	sweet chili sauce	30 mL
¼ cup	dark soy sauce	60 mL
pinch	turmeric	pinch
30	jumbo shrimp (21/25), peeled and deveined	30
6	lemongrass stalks, outer skins removed	6
to taste	kosher salt and white pepper	to taste

METHOD

Combine all the ingredients, except the shrimp and lemongrass, in a glass bowl. Add the shrimp. Stir to combine and refrigerate for 1 hour.

Preheat the grill to medium-high.

Using a sharp knife, cut points on the end of each lemongrass stalk. Skewer each shrimp (5 per lemongrass stalk) by running the lemongrass stalk from the tail end to the head so that each shrimp is in a letter U position. Season the shrimp with salt and pepper. Grill until the shrimp have turned pink and are cooked through, about 5 minutes per side. Serve with your favorite risotto.

CRAB

The crab that walks too far falls into the pot

—Haitian proverb

I WISH I COULD REMEMBER THE FIRST TIME I HAD CRAB. Although the memory escapes me, I'll always remember the best time, if not the first. I call it "The Feast of the Snow Crab."

When I was married, my husband suffered from pre-Christmas blues. Wanting to serve something festive on Christmas Eve to cheer him up, I mulled over the possibilities. Veal was one, but I would have to drive halfway across town to get it. That year there were four-foot-high drifts of snow, so I opted for crab, which I could get only two blocks away.

We were going to have it hot with a lemony mayonnaise, but then a moment of madness possessed us. We ran out to the backyard and placed the freshly cooked crabs in the snow. We almost choked we were laughing so hard, and Ginger the dog couldn't figure out whether to wag or sulk. In the weak spotlight made by the flashlight, we watched the crabs steaming serenely in the snow, and were awed by the reverence of the occasion. Snow Crab was born.

Chilled is an easy way to serve crab. You can take your time with it and not worry about warm crabmeat getting cold. Extracting a small mountain of meat and piling it onto a piece of toasted baguette with a slathering of fresh lemon mayonnaise is one of those moments when you realize what life can be all about. Large crabs (1¾–2 lb/875 g–1 kg) are ideal for eating as there is a bigger reward for the amount of cracking required.

There are many different crabs available worldwide but here we'll deal with those that are close to home: the Dungeness, and fresh or frozen crabmeat (since most of the recipes in this chapter use just the meat rather than whole crabs).

On the West Coast, the total catch of the Dungeness ranges from 35–55 million pounds annually. The Dungeness crab's Latin name, *Cancer magister*, simply means "master crab." The crab gets its common name from Dungeness, a small town in Washington State. The annual Dungeness Crab and Seafood Festival is held close by in Port Angeles, Washington, every October.

A crab's gender can be determined by the shape of its underside "apron." The male crab's apron is shaped like an inverted T. An adult female's apron is broad and rounded, while an immature female's is triangular. Only male crabs measuring at least 6¼ inches across the shell may be harvested, with all female and small males returned to the water to create healthy stocks for future harvest.

Fresh Dungeness meat is abundant on the West Coast, and it is sweet and succulent. Frozen Jonah and rock crabmeat is readily available. In my experience, rock crab is the superior of the two with its meat bearing a similarity to Dungeness crab. Frozen crabmeat should be slowly thawed in the fridge on a plate to catch the drips. Use within 2 days of thawing. Fresh crabmeat should be used the day it's purchased. Canned crabmeat is very convenient because it's ready when you are and comes in smaller sizes. It's good in a pinch, but nothing beats fresh crabmeat or a good-quality frozen meat.

Whether fresh, frozen, or canned, pick over the meat to remove any cartilage or fragments of shell before using.

Choosing, Cooking, and Cleaning Crab

Choosing a crab is fairly simple. Always buy from a live tank and make sure the crab is feisty. A limp-looking crab is either dead, or well on its way.

Bring a large pot of water to a boil, with enough water to completely submerge the crab(s) plus an additional 4 or 5 inches of water above the crab(s). Add ½ cup (125 mL) of kosher or sea salt for each gallon (4 L) water. Add the crab and place a lid on the pot. When the water starts to foam and lift the lid of the pot, turn off the heat and let the crab sit in the hot water for 5 minutes. Remove from the pot and serve, or clean first then serve, depending on your preference.

To clean a crab (use rubber gloves if the crab is hot), place the crab belly-side up on a flat surface. Lift and remove the belly flap, or "apron." Turn the crab over and remove the top shell by inserting your thumb between the body and shell at the rear of the crab and pulling the shell up. Remove the gills on either side of the body and the intestine which runs down the center of the back.

Most people wash away the "crab butter" which is the greenish matter in the cavity. It's quite tasty, so if you're adventurous, save it. It can be slathered on toasted baguette and eaten along with the crab or incorporated into a sauce for the crab.

Your crab is now cleaned and ready to eat. Cooked and cleaned crab can be stored covered and refrigerated for 2 days.

One pound (500 g) of crabmeat is approximately 2 cups (500 mL), lightly packed.

You can use canned, frozen, or fresh crabmeat to make these elegant, hot, and appetizing canapés. Makes 16–20 pieces.

HOT CRAB & ASPARAGUS CANAPÉS

INGREDIENTS

1	8 oz (225 g) package cream cheese, at room temperature	1
1 cup	crabmeat, drained and squeezed of excess moisture	250 mL
1	garlic clove, finely chopped	1
2	green onions, finely chopped	2
to taste	salt, lemon juice, and hot pepper sauce	to taste
16–20	¼-inch (6 mm) thick baguette slices	16–20
16–20	small asparagus spears, blanched and cut in half lengthwise	16–20
¼ cup	freshly grated Parmesan cheese	60 mL

METHOD

Preheat the oven to 400°F (200°C).

Beat the cream cheese until light. Beat in the crab, garlic, and green onion until just combined; season with salt, lemon juice, and hot pepper sauce. Spread the mixture on the baguette slices and then place the slices on a nonstick baking tray. Top each canapé with two half asparagus spears, cut side down, overlapping them slightly. Sprinkle with a little Parmesan cheese. Bake for 10 minutes or until heated through. Arrange on a platter and serve.

OPTION

These canapés can be made several hours in advance and stored, loosely wrapped, in the fridge. Because you'll be baking them cold, allow 3–4 minutes extra cooking time. Try replacing the crab with an equal amount of cooked salad shrimp, finely chopped.

This decadent dip, inspired by one of my favorite chefs, combines two old favorites in one rich, creamy concoction. Serve it warm with pita chips, French bread, or vegetables. Serves 4–6.

HOT CRAB & ARTICHOKE DIP

INGREDIENTS

1	4 oz (125 g) package fat-reduced cream cheese	1
2 Tbsp	bottled chili sauce	30 mL
1 tsp	freshly squeezed lemon juice	5 mL
1 tsp	prepared horseradish	5 mL
½ cup	low-fat mayonnaise	125 mL
½ cup	low-fat plain yogurt or sour cream	125 mL
1 cup	finely grated Parmesan or Romano cheese	250 mL
to taste	freshly ground black pepper	to taste
½ tsp	hot pepper sauce	2 mL
1	14 oz (398 mL) can artichoke hearts, drained well and chopped	1
1	garlic clove, chopped	1
1	green onion, chopped	1
1 cup	fresh, frozen, or canned crabmeat	250 mL
to garnish	paprika	to garnish

METHOD

Preheat the oven to 350°F (180°C).

In a food processor, add the cream cheese, chili sauce, lemon juice, horseradish, mayonnaise, yogurt, Parmesan, pepper, and hot pepper sauce. Process until smooth. Using a rubber spatula, scrape down the sides of the bowl so that all of the ingredients are well combined. Add the artichoke hearts, garlic, chopped green onions, and crabmeat (make sure to remove any bits of shell or cartilage). Pulse a few times, just to combine (not purée). Spoon the dip into a small baking dish, dust with paprika, and bake for 20–30 minutes or until it begins to bubble and starts to brown on top. Serve this dip hot, with pita chips or crostini.

TIP

You can make this dip in advance, cover, and chill overnight, then bake as needed.

A warm and creamy beginning for a memorable evening. For a larger group, double the ingredients. Serve with crackers, tortilla chips, or slices of baguette. Serves 4.

HOT HERBACEOUS CRAB DIP

INGREDIENTS

1 Tbsp	melted butter	15 mL
⅓ cup	bread crumbs	75 mL
½ lb	fresh crabmeat	250 g
¼ cup	finely chopped celery	60 mL
2 Tbsp	finely chopped red bell pepper	30 mL
1	shallot, finely chopped	1
1	green onion, finely chopped	1
2 tsp	fresh lemon juice	10 mL
¼ tsp	sea salt	1 mL
2 Tbsp	soft cream cheese	30 mL
¼ cup	mayonnaise	60 mL
1 tsp	Dijon mustard	5 mL
to taste	hot pepper sauce	to taste
1 Tbsp	finely chopped Italian parsley, half reserved to garnish	15 mL
½ tsp	finely chopped fresh rosemary	2 mL

METHOD

Preheat the oven to 350°F (180°C).

Combine the melted butter and bread crumbs in a small bowl. In a separate bowl, combine all the other ingredients. Place the mixture in a small, lightly buttered gratin dish or medium soufflé dish. Top with the bread crumb mixture and bake for approximately 10 minutes, until it's bubbling.

A potsticker is basically a small, filled dumpling that is browned in a pan and simmered in broth until tender. Dumpling wrappers, black sesame seeds, green pea shoots, and chili garlic sauce can be found in the Asian section of your supermarket. Makes 36 potstickers.

CRAB & PAPAYA POTSTICKERS
WITH CHILI SESAME OIL

INGREDIENTS

1 Tbsp	sesame oil	15 mL
2 Tbsp	minced shallot	30 mL
2 Tbsp	finely diced red bell pepper	30 mL
¾ cup	crabmeat	175 mL
½ cup	finely sliced papaya	125 mL
2 Tbsp	chopped fresh cilantro leaves	30 mL
1 tsp	ground coriander	5 mL
to taste	sea salt and freshly ground black pepper	to taste
1	½ lb (250 g) package round dumpling wrappers	1
for dusting	cornstarch	for dusting
3 Tbsp	canola oil	45 mL
1½ cups	chicken stock	375 mL
¾ cup	Chili Sesame Oil (see recipe next page)	175 mL
1 Tbsp	black sesame seeds, roasted	15 mL
1 oz	green pea shoots	25 g

METHOD

Heat the oil in a small saucepan over medium heat. Add the shallot and red pepper and sauté for about 2 minutes. Remove from the heat and let cool. In a bowl, combine the sautéed mixture with the crabmeat, papaya, cilantro, coriander, and salt and pepper.

Place a dumpling wrapper on your work surface and moisten the outside rim with a little water. Place about 1 tsp (5 mL) of filling in the center of the wrapper and fold it over to form a half circle. Pick it up and make about 4 pleats around the rim to seal the edge. Lightly dust a parchment-lined cookie sheet with cornstarch and place the dumplings on the sheet in a single layer. Make the remaining dumplings.

You will need to cook the dumplings in 2 or 3 batches, so divide the oil and chicken stock accordingly. Heat some of the canola oil in a large nonstick skillet and add the potstickers, placing them in a single layer.

Fry until they are browned, turn them over, and add some of the chicken stock. Cover and simmer for 3–4 minutes, or until tender. Repeat with the remaining dumplings.

To serve, arrange the potstickers in a circle on the plates, drizzle with the chili sesame oil, and garnish with black sesame seeds and green pea shoots.

Chili Sesame Oil
Makes ¾ cup (175 mL).

¼ cup	sesame oil	60 mL
¼ cup	canola oil	60 mL
2 Tbsp	chili garlic sauce	30 mL
1 Tbsp	soy sauce	15 mL
1 Tbsp	lime juice	15 mL

Put all the ingredients in a small bowl and stir to combine. This will keep for up to 2 weeks covered in the refrigerator.

Crab and avocado are a match made in heaven. This rich and inviting soup makes an elegant lunch or starter on a hot summer day. Serves 4.

CHILLED CRAB & AVOCADO SOUP

INGREDIENTS

2	medium avocados, quartered, pitted, and peeled	2
2½ cups	chicken or vegetable stock	625 mL
½ cup	light sour cream	125 mL
1	lime, juice of	1
2 tsp	curry powder	10 mL
to taste	salt	to taste
1 cup	crabmeat	250 mL
2 Tbsp	finely chopped yellow or red bell pepper	30 mL
2 Tbsp	chopped cilantro or green onion	30 mL

METHOD

Place the avocado, 1 cup (250 mL) of the stock, and the sour cream in a food processor or blender. Pulse until smooth, then transfer to a bowl. Stir in the remaining stock and the lime juice, curry powder, and salt. Chill the soup for at least 2 hours. Pour into chilled soup bowls. Divide the crabmeat among the bowls, setting it in the center of the soup. Sprinkle with the bell pepper and cilantro or green onion and serve.

Although I call this a chowder, it is not as thick and chunky as most. Cutting the vegetables very fine helps to highlight the crabmeat and gives a slightly more refined feel to the soup. For a less expensive version, substitute snow or Jonah crab for the Dungeness. Makes 8 cups (2 L).

DUNGENESS CRAB & CORN CHOWDER

INGREDIENTS

½ cup	butter	125 mL
¼ cup	finely diced onion	60 mL
1 Tbsp	minced garlic	15 mL
¼ cup	finely diced celery	60 mL
¼ cup	finely diced carrot	60 mL
¼ cup	finely diced red bell pepper	60 mL
¼ cup	finely diced fennel bulb	60 mL
½ cup	all-purpose flour	125 mL
¼ tsp	ground cumin	1 mL
½ tsp	ground coriander	2 mL
¼ tsp	cayenne pepper	1 mL
5 cups	cold fish stock	1.25 L
2 cups	frozen corn	500 mL
2 cups	Dungeness crabmeat	500 mL
½ cup	whipping cream (35%)	125 mL
1 tsp	lemon juice	5 mL
2 Tbsp	chopped cilantro	30 mL
1½ tsp	sea salt	7 mL

METHOD

Melt the butter in a medium pot over medium heat. Add the onion, garlic, celery, carrot, red pepper, and fennel and cook for 3 minutes, stirring often. Reduce the heat to low and add the flour, cumin, coriander, and cayenne pepper. Cook for 5 minutes, stirring often. Increase the heat to medium high and stir in the fish stock a third at a time. Once it comes to a boil add the corn, reduce the heat to a simmer, and cook for 5 minutes. Add the crabmeat, cream, lemon, cilantro, and salt. Cook for 2 more minutes. Serve immediately.

The chef at Merrill Inn in Picton, Ontario, likes to serve this perennial favorite over a bed of dressed greens. If you choose to, you could make these a little smaller and serve them as cocktail fare. Don't forget the tartar sauce and fresh lemon wedges. Serves 4–6.

CLASSIC CRAB CAKES

INGREDIENTS

1 lb	crabmeat (fresh or frozen)	500 g
1	large egg, lightly beaten	1
2 Tbsp	mayonnaise	30 mL
1 tsp	Dijon mustard	5 mL
1 tsp	Worcestershire sauce	5 mL
1 Tbsp	Old Bay seasoning	15 mL
½	small red onion, diced	½
1	celery stalk, diced	1
½	red bell pepper, diced	½
1 Tbsp	finely chopped chives	15 mL
½ cup	fresh bread crumbs	125 mL
to taste	salt and freshly ground black pepper	to taste
2 Tbsp	unsalted butter	30 mL
2 Tbsp	vegetable oil	30 mL

METHOD

Pick over the crabmeat to remove any shell or cartilage; pull it apart into chunks and set aside.

In a large bowl, combine the egg, mayonnaise, mustard, Worcestershire sauce, Old Bay seasoning, onion, celery, red pepper, and chives. Mix well, then add the bread crumbs, crabmeat, salt, and pepper. Using a fork, blend the ingredients together well. Divide the mixture into 8 equal portions (or smaller if you wish). Shape each one into a patty about 2 inches (5 cm) in diameter and about ¾ of an inch (2 cm) thick.

In a large frying pan, warm 1 Tbsp (15 mL) of the butter and 1 Tbsp (15 mL) of the oil over medium-high heat. Fry half of the crab cakes for about 4 minutes on each side until golden brown on both sides, turning once with a spatula. Repeat with the remaining butter, oil, and crab cakes. Serve immediately.

You're going to die when you make this. Not only is the appetizer delicious—it also looks très cool. The recipe calls for semifirm nutty sweet Asiago cheese, which acts as a great counterpoint to the crab. You can substitute mozzarella or any other cheese that is soft enough to melt easily but hard enough to help bind the cake. Serves 6.

ASIAGO & ANGEL HAIR PASTA CRAB CAKES

INGREDIENTS

10 oz	good-quality crabmeat, approximately 1½ cups (375 mL)	300 g
2 Tbsp	unsalted butter or olive oil	30 mL
2	garlic cloves, minced	2
2	shallots, finely diced	2
½ lb	angel hair pasta	250 g
2	eggs, beaten	2
¼ cup	finely chopped Italian parsley	60 mL
¼ cup	finely chopped fresh cilantro	60 mL
⅓ cup	Dijon mustard	75 mL
10 oz	Asiago cheese, grated	300 g
2 Tbsp	all-purpose flour	30 mL
½	red or yellow bell pepper, finely diced	½
to taste	salt and pepper	to taste
for frying	vegetable oil	for frying

METHOD

Pick over the crabmeat to remove any shell or cartilage; pull it apart into chunks and set aside.

Add the butter to a medium-sized skillet and melt over medium-high heat. Add the garlic and shallots and reduce the heat to medium. Cook until brown and caramelized. Watch the heat, or the garlic will burn and you will have to start all over.

Bring a large pot of salted water to a boil and add the pasta. Cook until al dente and drain. Let cool slightly but don't rinse, because you want the pasta a bit sticky.

Once the pasta is done, transfer the shallots and garlic to a large mixing bowl and add the eggs, parsley, cilantro, and mustard. Mix well and add the pasta. Mix some more. Use your hands. Get in there and feel your food. Be sure to wash your hands first though.

Add the cheese, flour, diced pepper, crabmeat, and salt and pepper and mix some more.

Add just enough vegetable oil to coat a large skillet and bring to medium-high heat until the oil is hot but not smoking. Using your hands, scoop up some of the crab cake mixture and form a tiny patty, just as you would do if you were making a small hamburger. Slide the crab cake into the oil and cook for about 3 minutes on each side or until crispy brown. Continue to add crab cakes to the skillet, but make sure you don't overcrowd or the cakes won't crisp up.

Transfer the finished cakes to paper towels to drain. Serve with a nice roasted red pepper and balsamic purée and chopped chives.

Sweet soy sauce is also known as *ketjap manis* and can be found in Asian grocery stores. Serves 4.

CRAB & SPINACH SALAD
WITH SOY-ONION AIOLI

INGREDIENTS

¼ cup	mayonnaise	60 mL
1 Tbsp	sweet soy sauce (ketjap manis)	15 mL
1 tsp	minced garlic	5 mL
1 tsp	chili sauce (or hot sauce to taste)	5 mL
1	green onion, minced	1
1 Tbsp	light oil	15 mL
1 Tbsp	minced garlic	15 mL
1 lb	spinach, washed	500 g
¼ lb	cooked crabmeat	125 g
1 Tbsp	toasted sesame seeds	15 mL

METHOD

To make the aioli, combine the mayonnaise, sweet soy sauce, garlic, chili sauce, and green onion in a mixing bowl. Whisk until smooth and set aside.

Sauté the oil and garlic in a large nonstick pan over medium-high heat, until sizzling. Add the spinach and toss until the leaves just wilt, about 1 minute. Add the crabmeat and sauté until heated through, about 1 minute.

Mound the salad on a serving platter. Drizzle the soy-onion aioli on top and around the greens. Garnish with sesame seeds and serve immediately.

Artist and designer, jeweler, music lover, and keen putterer-about in the kitchen, Robert Gerownow does his wonderful small-scale creations—custom fridge magnets that look like Russian religious icons, one-of-a-kind stamps, small shadow boxes—under the *nom d'art* Ghetto Primate. The following is his recipe. Serves 2.

RASPBERRY CRAB SALAD

INGREDIENTS

¼ cup	raspberry vinegar	60 mL
6 Tbsp	dry white wine	90 mL
¼ cup	olive oil	60 mL
1 Tbsp	mixed fine herbs	15 mL
4 Tbsp	liquid clover honey	60 mL
2 Tbsp	freshly grated Parmesan cheese	30 mL
1	lemon, zested, then quartered	1
1	large egg	1
⅓ lb	fresh crabmeat, plus 2 legs or claws	170 g
¼ cup	raspberries (drained, if frozen)	60 mL
¼ cup	sour cream	60 mL
1	large head butter lettuce	1

METHOD

In a large bowl, combine raspberry vinegar, white wine, olive oil, herbs, honey, Parmesan cheese, and half of the lemon zest. Mix well. Squeeze juice from one-quarter of the lemon into the mixture, add the egg, and whisk well. Gently fold in the crabmeat (reserving the legs or claws to garnish) and raspberries. Chill.

To make the sour cream garnish, mix the sour cream, the juice of a quarter lemon, a pinch of fine herbs, and a pinch of lemon zest in a small bowl.

Separate 2 perfect, large leaves from the head of lettuce and set aside on salad plates; these will be your salad bowls. Tear half the remaining lettuce into fork-friendly pieces in a big salad bowl. Add the vinaigrette and toss gently.

Place the salad into the butter leaf bowls. On top of each salad place a dollop of sour cream garnish and, on top of that, one crab leg or claw. Sprinkle the remaining lemon zest over both salads and serve at once.

Dungeness crab was another glorious reward for moving west. While I enjoy it chilled with a lemony mayonnaise, this recipe is for those of you who, like me, feel that digging into a drippy, savory crab transcends all other eating experiences. Serves 4 as an appetizer or 2 as a main course.

HERB & PARMESAN ROASTED DUNGENESS CRAB

INGREDIENTS

2	2 lb (1 kg) Dungeness crabs, freshly cooked	2
1½ tsp	fennel seeds, coarsely crushed	7 mL
½ cup	coarsely chopped parsley	125 mL
½ cup	coarsely chopped fresh basil leaves	125 mL
4	garlic cloves, minced	4
¼ tsp	cayenne pepper	1 mL
2 tsp	paprika	10 mL
½ tsp	sea salt	2 mL
1 tsp	freshly ground black pepper	5 mL
⅓ cup	extra virgin olive oil	75 mL
½ cup	freshly grated Parmesan cheese	125 mL

METHOD

Pull the top shells from the crabs and remove the gills and the soft matter in the middle. Cut the crabs in half and crack the legs.

Combine the fennel, parsley, basil, garlic, cayenne, paprika, salt, pepper, and olive oil. Place the crabs in a shallow baking dish that holds them comfortably in a single layer. Pour the herb mixture over the crabs and toss to coat them well. Cover and refrigerate for 2 hours.

Preheat the oven to 400°F (200°C). Sprinkle the crabs with the Parmesan cheese and roast on the top rack of the oven until golden brown, about 10 minutes. Serve immediately.

This sumptuous pudding with a peppery Dungeness crab filling can be easily made ahead of time for a special brunch. You don't have to wait till brunch though. It is wonderful at any meal! Serves 8.

CRAB & SPINACH BREAD PUDDING

INGREDIENTS

1 lb	fresh or frozen crabmeat	500 g		1	2 lb (1 kg) loaf of good quality unsliced white bread	1
1	10 oz (285 g) bag of washed baby spinach	1		6	large eggs	6
1 cup	finely diced onion	250 mL		2 Tbsp	Dijon mustard	30 mL
2	medium garlic cloves, minced	2		½ tsp	sea salt	2 mL
2 Tbsp	unsalted butter	30 mL			a few gratings of nutmeg	
½ tsp	sea salt	2 mL		6 cups	homogenized milk	1.5 L
¼ tsp	freshly ground black pepper	1 mL		½ lb	aged white cheddar or Asiago cheese, shredded	250 g
	a few gratings of nutmeg			1 Tbsp	unsalted butter	15 mL
a pinch	cayenne pepper	a pinch				

METHOD

Pick over the crabmeat, removing any bit of shell or cartilage. Place in a large bowl.

Place the spinach in a large pot. Cover and turn the heat to medium-high. Cook, stirring occasionally, until the spinach wilts. Drain and spread out onto a plate to cool. When the spinach has cooled, squeeze out the water and chop finely. Add to the crab.

Sauté the onion and garlic in the 2 Tbsp (30 mL) butter until translucent. Add the salt, pepper, nutmeg, and cayenne. Add to the crab and spinach mixture and mix well.

Trim the crusts from the bread and slice into 1-inch (2.5 cm) slices.

Beat the eggs, mustard, salt, and nutmeg together. Stir in the milk.

Generously butter a 9- x 13-inch (23 x 33 cm) baking pan. Fit one layer of bread, without overlapping, into the pan. Spread half of the grated cheese evenly over the bread. Spread the crab mixture evenly over the cheese then top with the remaining cheese. Lay the remaining bread over the crab mixture (you may overlap the bread if you wish).

Carefully pour the egg and milk mixture over the pudding, making sure that the top layer of bread is soaked with the egg and milk mixture. Let stand for 1 hour. Or, you can also cover and refrigerate the pudding overnight at this point. Bring to room temperature before baking.

Preheat the oven to 350°F (180°C). Bake the pudding for 30 minutes. Remove from the oven and spread the tablespoon of butter over the top. Return to the oven and bake for 30 minutes longer. Remove from the oven and let rest for 15 minutes before serving.

How decadent! A feast like this must really mean you have a reason to celebrate. Frozen Alaskan king crab legs come already cooked, so all you have to do is heat and dig in! Serves 2.

ALASKAN KING CRAB
WITH GRAND MARNIER BUTTER

INGREDIENTS

2 lb	frozen Alaskan king crab legs, thawed	1 kg
1	lemon, quartered	1
1	shallot, minced	1
½ cup	dry white wine	125 mL
2 Tbsp	Grand Marnier liqueur	30 mL
4 Tbsp	unsalted butter, diced and chilled	60 mL
to taste	coarse salt and ground black pepper	to taste

METHOD

Warm the crab legs and lemon in a roasting pan covered with foil for 20 minutes at 325°F (160°C).

Meanwhile, place the shallot and wine in a saucepan and reduce to ¼ cup (60 mL). Add the Grand Marnier and return to a simmer. Remove from the heat and whisk in the butter until a thick creamy consistency is achieved. Season to taste.

Serve the crab with sauce on the side in ramekins for dipping.

LOBSTER

A woman should never be seen eating or drinking,

unless it be lobster salad & Champagne, the only true

feminine & becoming viands.

—Lord Byron

ᔆ

WE WERE IN THE THROES OF NEWLY FOUND LOVE. He was going to the University of Toronto at the time, working as a dishwasher on the weekends and living on cottage cheese and sliced ham. I thought I was a bit more sophisticated as far as food was concerned, having cooked in restaurants for five years, and had progressed as far as ramen noodles. We thought we were truly in the know and would have small feasts of brie cheese, pâté, and French bread to prove it. It was time, though, for something truly special, something unique, to celebrate our union. Lobster and champagne it was! We would have a lobster feast on the roof of the house where I lived, gazing into the downtown skyscape of Toronto.

But, how do you buy a lobster and how do you cook it? Neither of us had cooked a whole lobster, so with great fear and excitement we chose and cooked them. While they were cooking, we painstakingly and carefully prepared the hollandaise and gingerly steamed a bunch of asparagus. We rushed—with our dinner—up three floors to the roof where pillows, blankets, and an electric lamp were set up. We toasted each other and toasted the city. I don't remember much about eating except scooping up the hollandaise with the lobster and marveling at its texture and flavor. What I do remember is that it was one of the sweetest, most romantic nights of my life. In that giddy, newly-in-love way, we decided to sleep on the roof that night, and several hours into sleep were awakened by drops of rain.

About Lobster

Now known as a luxury ingredient, lobster was once so abundant in parts of North America that it was considered very plain.

East Coast lobsters used to be so plentiful that they were often found on the beach at low tide. The Mi'kmaq and Malseet peoples of Atlantic Canada used them as food, fertilizer, and decorative material. With the arrival of European settlers, the abundant population of lobsters was viewed as "poor fare." Easily harvested from tidal pools, they were served to children, prisoners, and indentured servants. In Massachusetts, many servants rebelled and had clauses included in their contracts to ensure that they would not have to eat lobster more than three times a week.

By the 1840s, commercial fisheries were in full swing, and lobster caught the public's attention. Shipments of this tasty crustacean were spanning the globe, creating fans wherever they traveled. Lobster palaces became popular in major cities, where diners showed off their wealth by chowing down on several lobsters at a sitting.

The increased demand caused the stocks to dwindle due to overfishing, and by the 1940s, lobsters had climbed to the status of a delicacy. It was not rationed during World War II and the booming economy of wartime enabled people to splurge on small indulgences such as lobster. After the war, there was a decline in popularity but lobster consumption rapidly rebounded. Even though the size and population of the lobster has decreased, commercial lobster fishery is now carefully managed.

Canadian lobster is harvested twice a year, from April to June when the spring season opens, and then again in December after the winter fishery opens in southwestern Nova Scotia. At these times, the lobster is at its best. During the summer months and into the fall, the lobster molts, as well as mates. They shed their old shells while simultaneously absorbing water which expands their body size. As with other shellfish, you'll find that eating lobster is a lackluster experience during spawning. If you choose to eat lobster when spawning and find the meat shrunken and mushy, it's most likely the fault of the lobster, and not the person who cooked it. A lobster of minimum legal size will usually molt once per year and increase by approximately 15 percent in length and 40 percent in weight.

The largest lobster on record was caught in 1977 in Nova Scotia, weighing in at 44 pounds, 6 ounces and measuring nearly 4 feet long.

Storing and Preparing Live Lobster

I think the ideal size for lobster is between 1¾ and 2 lb (875 g to 1 kg) because the meat cooks quickly and evenly. Like crabs, lobsters should be lively when pulled from the live tank. The elastics around the claws are there for your protection so don't remove them until the lobster is cooked.

You can store live lobsters refrigerated and under a damp towel—where they'll remain calm—for up to one day.

The most common way of cooking lobster is by boiling, and here's how it's done:

Pour enough water to cover the lobster(s) completely into a very large pot. Add 1 Tbsp (15 mL) of sea salt for every quart (1 L) of water and bring to a rapid boil. Drop the lobster head first into the water and cover the pot with a lid. When the water returns to a boil, start timing. Boil the lobster for 10 minutes for the first pound of weight and then 3 more minutes for each extra pound. It doesn't matter how many lobsters are being cooked in the pot; the same timing applies. It's a good idea to choose lobsters of the same size if you're cooking them together. Drain the lobster immediately and serve hot or plunge into a bowl of ice to stop the cooking if you are going to serve it chilled.

Steaming is also a great way to cook lobster and some people think it's more flavorful than boiling. If you have a large steamer or can set up a trivet in a large pot, it's easy to do.

Place a few inches of water in a pot that you've set up for steaming or the bottom of a steamer, making sure that the water will not be touching the lobster. Bring the water to a rapid boil and place the lobsters on the steaming rack. Cook lobsters under 2 lb (1 kg) for 10–12 minutes, and those over 2 lb (1 kg) for 15–20 minutes. Again, it doesn't matter how many lobsters are steamed; the same timing applies.

Lobster tails should be thoroughly thawed in the refrigerator before cooking. Boil or steam the tails for 1 minute per ounce of weight. The tails curl up as they steam so if you want them straight, insert a wooden skewer lengthwise through the tail to keep them from curling.

If you need lobster meat for a certain recipe, shell immediately after cooling and store covered and refrigerated for up to 2 days.

Frozen lobster meat should be thawed completely in the fridge before using.

The lobster contains the soft, yellowish green liver, which is known as *tomalley*. This is delicious and can be incorporated into sauces. If you don't fancy tomalley, discard it.

I served this luscious soup to my wife when courting her with romantic dinners some 20 years ago. She said yes—what more do I need to say? Serves 4.

LOBSTER BISQUE

INGREDIENTS

1	1½ lb (750 g) cooked lobster	1
2 Tbsp	olive oil	30 mL
2	garlic cloves, sliced	2
1	small carrot, thinly sliced	1
1	celery rib, thinly sliced	1
1	small onion, thinly sliced	1
½ cup	dry white wine	125 mL
4 cups	lobster stock (see page 189), or fish stock	1 L
2 Tbsp	tomato paste	30 mL
1 tsp	dried tarragon	5 mL
1	bay leaf	1
3 Tbsp	all-purpose flour	45 mL
½ cup	whipping cream (35%)	125 mL
to taste	salt, white pepper, and cayenne pepper	to taste
2 oz	brandy	60 mL
1 Tbsp	chopped fresh parsley or chives	15 mL

METHOD

Cut the lobster in half lengthwise. Rinse out the cavity, and then pull out the tail meat. Crack the legs and claws and remove the meat. Thinly slice the lobster meat and set aside in the fridge.

Cut or break the shells into smaller pieces. Heat the oil in a pot over medium heat. Add the shells, garlic, carrot, celery, and onion and cook, stirring occasionally, for 5–6 minutes. Add the wine, 3½ cups (875 mL) of the stock, tomato paste, tarragon, and bay leaf. Bring to a gentle simmer and cook 30–40 minutes. Strain the lobster stock into another pot. Bring back to a simmer. Mix the flour with the remaining ½ cup (125 mL) of stock until it's smooth. Whisking steadily, slowly pour the mixture into the simmering stock. Gently simmer until the flour has cooked through and the soup has slightly thickened, about 5 minutes. Add the cream and reserved lobster. Season with salt, pepper, and cayenne.

Divide the brandy among 4 heated soup bowls. When the lobster is heated through, ladle the bisque into bowls, sprinkle with parsley or chives, and serve.

OPTION

To make crab bisque, replace the lobster with a whole, cooked Dungeness or snow crab weighing 1–1½ lb (500–750 g). Crack the shells and remove as much meat as you can. Rinse out the cavity. Cut or break the shells into smaller pieces and proceed as described for lobster bisque.

Everyone gets excited when lobster is brought to the table. An appetizer course is a great way to offer your guests a decadent treat without first having to get a bank loan. This salad is a wonderful shock of color. If lobster is too rich for you, use a few shrimp instead. This salad is a good reason to take the time to individually plate. The result is that everyone will get to enjoy the same amount of lobster. Serves 12.

LOBSTER MANGO SALAD
WITH LIME & CORIANDER

INGREDIENTS

6	1½ lb (750 g) live lobsters	6
2 Tbsp	coarse salt	30 mL
3	ripe mangoes	3
4	limes, quartered	4
1 cup	mayonnaise	250 mL
1 cup	thinly sliced green onions	250 mL
⅓ cup	chopped fresh coriander	75 mL
to taste	coarse salt and ground black pepper	to taste
12 cups	washed Boston or butter lettuce	3 L
for drizzling	extra virgin olive oil	for drizzling

METHOD

Bring a large pot of water to a boil and add 2 Tbsp (30 mL) of salt. Dunk 2 lobsters completely into the water, turn off the heat, cover, and let stand 10 minutes; remove the lobsters and allow to cool completely. Return the pot to the boil and repeat with the remaining lobsters, 2 at a time.

Shell the lobsters, working over a tray or large bowl. Cut all the meat into bite-sized pieces and refrigerate.

Peel, slice, and dice the mangoes. Squeeze around the pit to remove any extra pulp. Mix the mango pulp with the mayonnaise, the juice of 2 limes, green onion, and coriander. Toss the dressing with the lobster and season to taste.

To plate, arrange the lettuce on plates and drizzle with olive oil. Spoon the lobster onto the salad greens and serve with wedges of remaining lime.

I arrived home one day to find a pair of coolers on my front porch, each cooler jammed full of lobsters. In the face of such largesse from my friend Holly, I made a celebration salad. You can also use cooked monkfish, shrimp, leftover grilled halibut, or poached sablefish instead. Gourmet food stores carry vanilla vinegar, or you can make your own. Serves 6–8.

SUMMER SALAD
WITH NEW POTATOES & BEANS (& LOBSTER!)

INGREDIENTS

5	1 lb (500 g) cooked lobsters	5
2 lb	new Bintje potatoes	1 kg
½ lb	green or yellow beans	250 g
4	ears corn, cooked	4
¼ cup	finely minced red onion	60 mL
¼ cup	minced chives	60 mL
1 Tbsp	minced fresh lemon thyme or thyme	15 mL
1 Tbsp	minced fresh oregano	15 mL
2 Tbsp	orange-infused olive oil	30 mL
4 Tbsp	best-quality olive oil	60 mL
2 Tbsp	Vanilla Vinegar (see recipe next page)	30 mL
2 Tbsp	Japanese rice vinegar	30 mL
to taste	kosher salt and freshly cracked black pepper	to taste
to garnish	Caramelized Pecans (see recipe next page)	to garnish
to garnish	chive stalks and blossoms (optional)	to garnish

METHOD

Crack and shell the lobsters. Freeze the shells to make bisque on another day. Chop the lobster meat into bite-size bits. Cut the potatoes into halves or quarters and cook in salted water until tender. Drain and keep warm.

Tip and tail the beans (or not!) and steam them until just tender. Drain and refresh with cold water to set the color and stop the cooking process. Strip the corn kernels from the ears of corn.

Combine the shellfish and vegetables with the herbs, oils, and vinegars. Season with salt and pepper. Toss gently. Arrange on plates. Garnish with a sprinkle of pecans and fresh chives, if desired.

Caramelized Pecans
Makes about 2 cups (500 mL).

There is nothing shy about these sugar-coated nuts. They are the best midday snack, the best pizza topping, the best salad garnish, the best accompaniment to a glass of wine. Don't be tempted to sample them straight out of the pan—that melted sugar is hot enough to seriously burn your mouth. Let them cool and crisp before sampling.

2 cups	pecan halves	500 mL
2 Tbsp	unsalted butter	30 mL
2 Tbsp	sugar	30 mL
½ tsp	ground star anise	2 mL
½ tsp	cayenne	2 mL
to taste	kosher salt	to taste

Put the nuts in a colander or strainer and pour boiling water over them to minimize the tannins in the skin. Drain well, then place the nuts along with the remaining ingredients in a sauté pan. Cook over medium-high heat for about 7 minutes, stirring well, until the nuts are dark and glossy. Spread them out in a single layer on a baking sheet and cool.

Vanilla Vinegar

Infusing vinegar is an easy and quick way to transfer flavors. The intoxicating scent and taste of vanilla adds unexpected nuances to savory dishes, especially asparagus, lobster, and mixed greens. Choose a fairly mild, neutral vinegar you enjoy such as Japanese rice or champagne vinegar. Split 2 or 3 vanilla pods lengthwise, scrape out the seeds, then drop both into the bottle of vinegar. Cover, label, and let stand for a month before using.

I call this "almost" lobster thermidor because, unlike traditional recipes for the dish, which call for egg yolks and buckets of cream, this lighter version uses no egg yolk and only ½ cup (125 mL) of cream. Serve this refined dish on special occasions, such as Valentine's Day or Monday night. Serves 2.

ALMOST LOBSTER THERMIDOR FOR TWO

INGREDIENTS

1	1½ lb (750 g) live lobster	1
1 Tbsp	butter	15 mL
⅓ lb	mushrooms, thinly sliced	170 g
1	garlic clove, finely chopped	1
¼ tsp	paprika	1 mL
¼ tsp	dried tarragon	1 mL
1 oz	dry sherry	30 mL
½ cup	whipping cream (35%)	125 mL
to taste	salt and white pepper	to taste
2–3 Tbsp	freshly grated Parmesan cheese	30–45 mL

METHOD

Bring 1 gallon (4 L) of water to a boil. Add 2 Tbsp (30 mL) of salt to the pot. Add the lobster, return to a boil, and cook for 3 minutes, or until slightly underdone. Remove from the pot, drain well, and place on a tray. When the lobster is cool enough to handle, twist off the claws, crack them, and carefully remove the meat. Cut the lobster in half lengthwise, beginning from the tail end. Remove the tail meat. Cut all the lobster meat into ¼-inch (6 mm) pieces, and place on a plate. Rinse out the two shell halves of the lobster and pat dry. Place cut side up in a baking dish and set aside.

Preheat the oven to 425°F (220°C). Melt the butter in a skillet over medium heat. Add the mushrooms and cook until they're tender and the liquid has evaporated. Add the garlic, paprika, and tarragon and cook for 1 minute more. Add the sherry and cook until it has almost evaporated. Add the whipping cream and reduce until the mixture thickens lightly. Stir in the reserved lobster meat and remove from the heat. Season with salt and pepper.

Mound the lobster mixture into the lobster shells. Sprinkle with Parmesan cheese. Bake for 10–12 minutes, until golden and just heated through.

This is a wonderful, decadent, make-ahead meal that's perfect for a holiday dinner party—I created it for a New Year's celebration. Individual oval ramekins make perfect lasagnas for one, but you can also make it in a single pan, then chill, cut, and reheat for easy service. Try using no-boil lasagna noodles if fresh sheets are not available. Serves 4.

INDIVIDUAL LOBSTER LASAGNAS
WITH TWO CHEESES

INGREDIENTS

Lobster Sauce

1	medium fennel bulb	1
1 Tbsp	olive oil	15 mL
1 Tbsp	butter	15 mL
1	medium white onion, minced	1
1	medium carrot, finely diced	1
1	garlic clove, minced	1
2 Tbsp	cognac	30 mL
1 cup	chopped fresh or canned tomatoes	250 mL
1 Tbsp	tomato paste	15 mL
1 cup	fish or lobster stock (see page 189)	250 mL
½ cup	dry white wine	125 mL
¼ tsp	crushed saffron	1 mL
¼ cup	whipping cream (35%)	60 mL
2 cups	cooked lobster meat, chopped	500 mL
to taste	salt and white pepper	to taste

Béchamel Sauce

1½ cups	milk	375 mL
1 cup	whipping cream (35%)	250 mL
pinch	white pepper	pinch
big pinch	nutmeg	big pinch
big pinch	dried basil	big pinch
3 Tbsp	butter	45 mL
⅓ cup	all-purpose flour	75 mL
½ cup	grated Parmesan cheese	125 mL

For Assembly

1 lb	fresh lasagna sheets, cut into sixteen 3- x 5- inch (8 x 12 cm) rectangles	500 g
4 oz	dry Friulano cheese, shredded	125 g
2 oz	Parmesan cheese, shredded	50 g

METHOD

To make the lobster sauce, cut off the long stems and fronds of the fennel and peel the outer layer from the bulb. Finely slice the fennel, reserving some of the fronds for garnish.

Heat the oil and butter in a deep skillet and sauté the fennel, onion, and carrot for five minutes, until almost tender. Add the garlic and cognac and simmer until most of the liquid has evaporated. Stir in the tomatoes, tomato paste, stock, wine, and saffron. Simmer until the sauce has been reduced by half.

Add the cream and simmer 5 minutes longer, until the sauce thickens. Stir in the lobster, and season to taste with salt and pepper. Remove the sauce from the heat and keep warm.

To make béchamel, bring the milk, cream, pepper, nutmeg, and basil to a boil, then remove from the heat and set aside. Heat the butter until foamy, stir in the flour, and cook for 2 minutes. Gradually stir in the hot milk mixture, raise the heat, and simmer until thick and smooth. Stir in the Parmesan cheese.

Meanwhile, bring a pot of salted water to a boil and cook the pasta al dente, about 2–3 minutes. Drain and chill in cold water, then drain again.

In a bowl, combine the two cheeses.

Preheat the oven to 375°F (190°C). Place a little of the sauce in the bottom of four 4- to 5-inch (10–12 cm) round or square ovenproof dishes. Top with a sheet of pasta and a layer of the lobster sauce. Add a dollop of béchamel. Sprinkle lightly with the cheeses and add another layer of pasta. Continue layering sauce, cheese, and pasta, until each individual lasagna has four layers, ending with the pasta. Sprinkle the tops with more cheese. Place the individual lasagnas in the oven and bake for 7–8 minutes, just until bubbling and beginning to brown. Garnish each with the reserved fennel fronds and serve immediately.

Few things are as good as a steaming bowl of homemade macaroni and cheese, especially when it doesn't come out of a box! I don't normally put lobster in mine—and this version is great without my favorite crustacean—but it's a delicious way to make the ordinary extraordinary! Serves 4–6.

MAC & CHEESE WITH LOBSTER

INGREDIENTS

1	1 lb (500 g) box of penne pasta	1
1	4 oz (125 g) stick of butter	1
2	garlic cloves, chopped	2
⅔ cup	flour	150 mL
big splash	white wine	big splash
1	12 oz (357 mL) can of evaporated milk	1
4 cups	milk	1 L
1 Tbsp	paprika	15 mL
2–3 Tbsp	Dijon mustard	30–45 mL
pinch	cayenne pepper	pinch
1 lb	aged cheddar cheese, grated	500 g
sprinkle	salt	sprinkle
2 or 3	lobsters, about 1 lb (500 g) each, steamed, shelled, and chopped	2 or 3
half a loaf	Italian bread, hand-torn into small pieces	half a loaf
splash	olive oil	splash

METHOD

Preheat your oven to 350°F (180°C). Meanwhile, cook the pasta in lots of boiling, well-salted water. Cook the pasta until it's tender but still firm at the center; it will finish cooking in the sauce. Drain it well but don't rinse.

Melt the butter in a saucepan over medium heat, add the garlic and stir for several minutes as it softens and flavors the butter. Add the flour and stir with a wooden spoon until a smooth paste forms (the roux). Continue cooking a few more minutes as the roux toasts and develops a bit of flavor. Slowly stir in the wine and continue mixing until the mixture is smooth again. Continue whisking until the mixture is very thick, a few minutes longer. Stir in the paprika, Dijon, cayenne, cheese, and salt.

Stir the lobster meat into the cheese mixture along with the pasta. Pour everything into a 9- x 13-inch (23 x 33 cm) ovenproof baking dish. Toss the bread with a bit of

olive oil, then sprinkle it evenly over the top of the mixture. Bake until the casserole is heated through and the
bread crumbs are golden brown, about 30 minutes.

OPTION

*Try substituting other semifirm cheese, like Swiss, Jack, or
Emmenthal, for the cheddar. Just about any minced fresh herb
will add a wonderful aroma to the cheese sauce; I like thyme,
tarragon, and dill. You can replace the lobster with a can or
two of clams or a bag of shrimp. If you use clams, replace some
of the milk with their juice.*

TIP

*Combining the flour and butter into a roux helps evenly
distribute the flour throughout the sauce, preventing lumps.
Aged cheddar cheese adds much more flavor than a blander
mild cheddar.*

Toasted bread crumbs sprinkled over pasta originated in Southern Italy as an economical substitute for cheese. This particular recipe came about due to an overabundance of lobsters and tomatoes left over after a dinner party. For this dish to turn out at its best, it is imperative to undercook the pasta. It will continue cooking in the sauce. Serves 4.

SPAGHETTI

WITH LOBSTER, CHERRY TOMATOES & TOASTED BREAD CRUMBS

INGREDIENTS

⅔ cup	fresh, coarse white or Calabrese bread crumbs	150 mL
1 Tbsp	olive oil	15 mL
2	2 lb (1 kg) cooked, shelled lobsters, with meat cut into 1-inch (2.5 cm) pieces	2
¾ lb	spaghetti	375 g
2 Tbsp	olive oil	30 mL
20	red cherry tomatoes	20
10	yellow cherry tomatoes	10
3	garlic cloves, finely minced	3
1 Tbsp	finely chopped chives	15 mL
1 Tbsp	unsalted butter	15 mL
to taste	salt and freshly ground pepper	to taste

METHOD

Sauté the bread crumbs in olive oil until golden brown, and set aside.

Bring a large pot of salted water to a boil. Cook the pasta for about 7–8 minutes. It should be underdone. Drain and reserve 1 cup (250 mL) of the water.

While the pasta is cooking, heat the olive oil in a large sauté pan until it shimmers, then add the tomatoes. Lower the heat to medium and sauté the tomatoes for 1 minute. Add the garlic and a pinch of salt and pepper, and cook for about 2–3 minutes. Remove from the heat and add the lobster.

Return the sauté pan to medium heat, add the spaghetti and ⅓ cup (75 mL) of the reserved water, and toss gently. Add another ⅓ cup to ⅔ cup (75–150 mL) of the reserved water and the chives. Toss again. Add the butter, and salt and pepper if needed. Place in a heated bowl and sprinkle generously with the toasted bread crumbs.

I had a sous-chef named John A. MacDonald at my restaurant. No joke, although he took hundreds of them over his patriotic naming. John A. was a Cape Breton boy, and he loved telling stories about life "back home." He traded away lobster sandwiches for peanut butter and jelly. It was beyond my comprehension until he explained that to him and many other East Coasters, lobster was a food of last resort. Serves 4.

LOBSTER FOR JOHN A.

INGREDIENTS

1 Tbsp	unsalted butter	15 mL
½	sweet onion, diced	½
2 Tbsp	grated fresh ginger	30 mL
1	zucchini, diced	1
1–2 tsp	curry powder	5–10 mL
¼ cup	dry white wine	60 mL
1	lemon, juice and zest of	1
2 Tbsp	whipping cream (35%)	30 mL
1 lb	cooked lobster tail, sliced	500 g
3	green onions, diced	3
1	ripe mango, peeled and diced	1
to taste	kosher salt and freshly cracked black pepper	to taste
to garnish	roasted peanuts	to garnish

METHOD

Melt the butter in a sauté pan. Add the onions and ginger and cook over medium heat until the onion is tender, about 5–7 minutes. Add the zucchini and curry powder and stir well, cooking for several more minutes. Add the wine and lemon juice and zest and bring to a boil. Stir in the cream and the lobster. Heat thoroughly, adding a little cream or water if the pan gets too dry before the lobster is reheated. Stir in the green onions and mango, then adjust the seasoning with salt and pepper. Garnish with roasted peanuts.

So you indulge yourself with a big lobster feed. Well, don't throw the shells out when you're done. Wrap them up and stick them in the freezer until it's time for your next chichi dinner party. The shells and carcasses hold lots more lobster flavor than the meat does —they are the basis for this rich layered stock, which in turn makes a decadent Lobster Bisque (see page 174). Makes about 6 cups (1.5 L).

LOBSTER STOCK

INGREDIENTS

4	lobster carcasses and shells	4
for drizzling	olive oil	for drizzling
1	onion, medium dice	1
1	carrot, medium dice	1
1	celery stick, medium dice	1
¼ cup	olive oil	60 mL
2 Tbsp	tomato paste	30 mL
2 Tbsp	all-purpose flour	30 mL
¼ cup	brandy	60 mL
7 cups	fish stock or water	1.75 L
handful	parsley stalks	handful
6	tarragon sprigs	6
to taste	salt and pepper	to taste

METHOD

Preheat the oven to 375°F (190°C).

Take the lobster carcasses and remove everything inside, as it would lend a bitter taste to the stock if roasted. Wrap the shells in a dish towel and whack away with a meat tenderizer or the back of a big chef's knife until the shells are broken into smaller bits.

Put the pieces in a roasting pan and drizzle with olive oil. Cook in the oven until almost caramelized, about 30 minutes or so.

Remove the shells from the oven. Place in a pot and add the onion, carrot, and celery, and ¼ cup (60 mL) olive oil. Cook on the stovetop over medium-high heat until the onion is translucent, stirring every now and then.

Add the tomato paste and flour and cook for another two minutes or until the flour browns slightly and makes a bit of a paste.

Recipe continues on the next page . . .

Use the brandy to deglaze the roasting pan. Scrape the bottom of the pan to gather all the little bits of lobster, and add to the pot.

Top the carcasses with the fish stock (or water) and bring to a simmer. Add the parsley and tarragon and cook for 1 hour, skimming impurities.

Sieve the stock, discarding the bones and keeping the liquid. Season with salt and pepper.

TIP

Lobster butter is great drizzled over beef and fish. Simply take 1 cup (250 mL) of roasted shells, smash up, and add to a pot with 1 cup (250 mL) of butter. Simmer until fragrant. Add brandy to taste, and strain.

MIXED GRILL

Do not overcook this dish.
Most seafoods should simply be threatened
with heat then celebrated with joy.
—Jeff Smith, *The Frugal Gourmet*

❧

While most of us would think it odd to have a dish featuring chicken, beef, and pork, we melt over combinations of prawns, scallops, clams, mussels, oysters, crab, and lobster. There's something exciting, yet comforting at the same time, in choosing what tasty morsel you are going to eat next.

Paella, bouillabaisse, and cioppino are all wonderful dishes, but what really gets my tail wagging is gumbo. For a period in the '80s, Cajun food was all the rage. Every time I turned around, it seemed like I was bumping into another blackened something-or-other and everyone owned a copy of Paul Prudhomme's *Louisiana Kitchen*. Blackened everything aside, the one great dish that settled into my repertoire was gumbo. Shopping for the crab, oysters, prawns, sausage, and okra was exhilarating, and the cooking became an all-day event. I would spend an few hours shopping, another hour prepping the ingredients, an hour carefully stirring the roux, and another hour simmering the gumbo before the seafood went in. Served with Louisiana pecan rice and a well-chilled potato salad, this was one of the high points of eating; the gumbo was silky with fiery heat, the seafood sweet, and the potato salad took the spice off your tongue and got you ready to sink again into the depths of the dish.

One of my favorite restaurants in Toronto continues to be Boba, on Avenue Road. Bob Berman and Barbara Gordon's cozy place remains at the top of the list for solid satisfaction because these two can cook like crazy. I asked them for a recipe for my column in *NUVO* magazine a couple of years ago and was surprised—but delighted—when they sent this one. It's become my standard for crab cakes. Serves 6–8.

BOBA SEAFOOD CAKES
WITH TROPICAL TARTAR SAUCE

INGREDIENTS

1 lb	fresh crabmeat	500 g
½ lb	fresh scallops, diced	250 g
¼ lb	shrimp, peeled and cut into small pieces	125 g
1 Tbsp	chopped fresh chives	15 mL
1 Tbsp	chopped fresh parsley	15 mL
1 tsp	chopped fresh dill	5 mL
1 Tbsp	Dijon mustard	15 mL
1	medium potato, peeled, cooked, and mashed	1
to taste	salt and pepper	to taste
1 cup	finely ground homemade dry bread crumbs	250 mL
for frying	vegetable oil and unsalted butter	for frying

METHOD

In a large bowl, combine the seafood with the chives, parsley, and dill.

In a separate bowl, blend the mustard into the potatoes gently, and then carefully add it to the seafood mixture. Season with salt and pepper, form into 1-inch-thick (2.5 cm) cakes.

Put the bread crumbs on a plate and coat the cakes on both sides. Let rest for half an hour or longer in the fridge.

Heat ¼ inch (6 mm) of vegetable oil with 1 Tbsp (15 mL) of unsalted butter in a heavy frying pan. Working in batches so as not to crowd the cakes, cook until a golden crust forms and the seafood is cooked, about 4–5 minutes. Drain on paper towels.

Serve with tartar sauce (see recipe next page).

Tartar Sauce

Makes about 1 cup (250 mL).

1 cup	mayonnaise	250 mL
2 Tbsp	fresh lime juice	30 mL
2 Tbsp	minced green onions	30 mL
¼ cup	roasted sweet peppers (mix of red, yellow, and green)	60 mL
1 Tbsp	Caribbean hot sauce (Bob uses Matouk's Flambeau Sauce)	15 mL
to taste	salt and pepper	to taste

Blend all the ingredients together, seasoning with salt and pepper. Leave at least 2 hours to marinate.

This Mediterranean seafood salad can be served as a cold course to start a summer dinner party or as the main dish for your picnic. Serves 6–8.

MARINATED SEAFOOD SALAD

INGREDIENTS

1	small red onion, cut into thin rings	1
¾ lb	calamari tubes, cut into ¼-inch (6 mm) rings	375 g
¾ lb	medium shrimp, peeled and deveined	375 g
1 lb	mussels, scrubbed and debearded	500 g
¼ cup	extra virgin olive oil	60 mL
2	garlic cloves, crushed	2
¼ cup	freshly squeezed lemon juice	60 mL
½ tsp	Asian chili paste	2 mL
½ tsp	salt	2 mL
¼ tsp	freshly ground black pepper	1 mL
2 tsp	finely grated lemon rind	10 mL
⅓ cup	sliced pitted black olives	75 mL
¼ cup	finely sliced fresh basil leaves	60 mL
to garnish	fresh salad greens	to garnish

METHOD

In a small bowl of ice water, soak the sliced onion for 1 hour. Meanwhile, bring a large pot of salted water to a boil. Add the sliced calamari and simmer for 1 minute. Drain the calamari and immediately plunge it into ice water. Drain and set aside. Cook the shrimp in the same manner and set aside. Place the mussels in a large pot with a splash of water. Cover and steam over high heat for a few minutes until all the shells have opened. Remove the meat from the shells.

To make the dressing, combine the olive oil and garlic in a medium bowl. Set aside for 10 minutes. Whisk in the lemon juice and chili paste.

Drain the onion rings well and combine with the calamari, shrimp, and mussels in a glass bowl. Toss with the dressing, salt, pepper, lemon rind, and olives. Marinate in the refrigerator for several hours or overnight. Just before serving, stir in the fresh basil. Line a platter with greens and serve the seafood salad in the center.

Instead of buying whole lobsters, crabs, or shrimp, ask your fishmonger or a local restaurant to save shells for you. Most vendors will provide shells free of charge to regular customers. Serves 6.

SHELLFISH BISQUE

INGREDIENTS

1½ lb	raw lobster or shrimp shells, or a combination of the two, smashed into small pieces	750 g
2 Tbsp	unsalted butter	30 mL
1	onion, chopped	1
2	carrots, chopped	2
2	celery stalks, chopped	2
½ cup	brandy	125 mL
1	5½ oz (156 mL) can tomato paste	1
½ cup	all-purpose flour	125 mL
4 cups	fish stock	1 L
4 cups	chicken stock	1 L
1 tsp	caraway seed	5 mL
1	bay leaf	1
½ cup	whipping cream (35%)	125 mL
1 tsp	vanilla extract	5 mL
to taste	salt and freshly ground black pepper	to taste

METHOD

Melt the butter in a large saucepan. Add the onion, carrots, and celery; cook on medium-low heat for about 10 minutes or until very soft.

Add the crushed shells and continue cooking, stirring frequently, for 3 minutes or until the color changes. Do not scorch! Increase the heat to medium. Deglaze with brandy and bring to a boil. Stir in the tomato paste and cook, stirring often, for 5 minutes. Continue to stir constantly while dusting the mixture with the flour, adding a little stock if the mixture begins to scorch. Cook, stirring for 5 minutes; gradually add the fish and chicken stocks, caraway seed, and bay leaf.

Bring the mixture to a boil. Reduce the heat to low and simmer for 45 minutes. Discard the bay leaf and purée the bisque in a blender. Strain and return the bisque to the stove; bring to a boil. Whisk in the cream and vanilla and simmer for 3 minutes. Season with salt and pepper to taste.

These shellfish kabobs are great either as an appetizer or an entrée served over rice or couscous. Serves 4.

PESTO SHRIMP & SCALLOPS KABOBS

INGREDIENTS

16	medium scallops	16
16	extra large shrimp (26/30)	16
16	cherry tomatoes	16
1 cup	fresh basil leaves, packed	250 mL
2 Tbsp	grated Parmesan cheese	30 mL
1 Tbsp	toasted pine nuts	15 mL
1 oz	low-fat cream cheese	30 g
1 tsp	minced garlic	5 mL
3 Tbsp	chicken stock or water	45 mL
2 Tbsp	olive oil	30 mL
8	6-inch (15 cm) wooden skewers	8

METHOD

Place the wooden skewers in water for at least 30 minutes to prevent them from burning. Thread the scallops, shrimps, and tomatoes evenly onto the skewers.

To make the basil pesto, purée the basil, Parmesan, pine nuts, cream cheese, garlic, stock, and oil until smooth in the bowl of a small food processor. Brush half over the kabobs.

Grill or sauté in a nonstick skillet sprayed with vegetable spray until cooked on both sides, about 5 minutes. Serve with the remaining pesto.

A great party food—crispy textures with the great tastes of basil and seafood. Serves 4.

SEAFOOD TEMPURA SKEWERS
WITH LEMON CREAM DIP

INGREDIENTS

4	jumbo shrimp (16/20)	4
4	large scallops	4
1	bulb fennel	1
1	large red pepper	1
4 cups	Tempura Batter (see recipe next page)	1 L
8	large fresh basil leaves	8
	vegetable oil for deep-frying	
to taste	salt	to taste
8	6-inch (15 cm) wooden skewers	8
1½ cups	Lemon Cream Dip (see recipe next page)	375 mL

METHOD

Place the wooden skewers in water for at least 30 minutes to prevent them from burning. Meanwhile, peel and devein the shrimp, then cut in half lengthwise. Cut the scallops in half. Cut the fennel and red pepper into 1-inch (2.5 cm) squares. Assemble the skewers, using only one half of the skewer in the following order: half a scallop, basil leaf, fennel, a half shrimp, basil leaf, and red pepper. Repeat on all 8 skewers.

Prepare the Tempura Batter (see recipe next page).

Preheat oil in a deep fryer to 350°F (180°C). Dip the prepared skewers, one by one, in the tempura batter and deep-fry for 3–5 minutes. To remove any excess oil, drain on paper towels. Season immediately with salt.

For an effective presentation, push the finished skewers into a fresh pineapple, a Chinese eggplant, a daikon radish, or just let your imagination take over. Serve with the Lemon Cream Dip (see recipe next page).

Tempura Batter

Makes about 4 cups (1 L).

1 cup	cornstarch	250 mL
1 cup	flour	250 mL
2 tsp	salt	10 mL
1 tsp	cayenne pepper	5 mL
1 tsp	sesame seed oil	5 mL
¾ cup	ice-cold carbonated water	175 mL
½ cup	white wine	125 mL

Place all the dry ingredients into a bowl and lightly whisk until blended. Continue whisking and slowly add the oil, water, and wine, until smooth. Let rest for 15 minutes. Place the mixing bowl in a bowl of ice to keep the batter chilled until ready to use. The ice-cold carbonated water will help to achieve a light, crispy batter.

Lemon Cream Dip

Makes 1½ cups (375 mL).

This is a tangy, thick, and creamy dipping sauce, great with seafood, smoked fish, or chicken.

1 cup	sour cream	250 mL
¼ cup	lemon juice	60 mL
½ cup	chopped fresh chives	125 mL
¼ cup	grainy mustard	60 mL
to taste	salt and white pepper	to taste

Mix all the ingredients together. This dip can be stored in the refrigerator for 3–4 days.

Sole is one of the few fish difficult to overbake. This is a plus for those intimidated by cooking fish. Stuffing it with a tasty filling brings out more flavor. *Serves 4.*

SOLE ROLLED
WITH CRAB & GARLIC BREAD CRUMBS

INGREDIENTS

4 oz	crabmeat	125 g
2 Tbsp	low-fat mayonnaise	30 mL
1 Tbsp	freshly squeezed lemon juice	15 mL
¼ cup	chopped green onions	60 mL
2 Tbsp	chopped dill	30 mL
2 Tbsp	seasoned bread crumbs, store-bought	30 mL
1 tsp	olive oil	5 mL
½ tsp	crushed garlic	2 mL
1½ lb	sole fillets	750 g
2 Tbsp	chopped parsley	30 mL

METHOD

Preheat the oven to 425°F (220°C). Spray a baking dish with vegetable spray.

To make the crab stuffing, combine the crabmeat, mayonnaise, lemon juice, green onion, and dill in the bowl of a food processor. Pulse until the mixture is combined, but still chunky. Alternatively, you can finely chop all of the ingredients by hand.

In a bowl, combine the bread crumbs, oil, and garlic.

Spoon the crab stuffing onto the sole fillets, dividing the stuffing evenly between the portions. Roll them up and fasten with a toothpick. Sprinkle the crumb mixture overtop. Place in the prepared baking dish and bake for 10 minutes or until just cooked. Garnish with parsley.

Here's a classy meal to make the first night out on the trail (or to celebrate when you've arrived at an isolated cabin). If the seafood is frozen when you leave, it will be nicely thawed and ready to steam on the open fire. Now's the time to pour that Sauvignon Blanc you hauled in. Serves 4.

CAMPFIRE SEAFOOD BAKE

INGREDIENTS

4	18-inch (45 cm) squares of heavy aluminum foil	4
16	small new red potatoes, halved or quartered	16
1	large onion, thinly sliced	1
2 or 3	ears of fresh corn, cut into 2-inch (5 cm) pieces	2 or 3
16	mussels, scrubbed and debearded	16
16	large shrimp, peeled and deveined	16
2 Tbsp	chopped fresh parsley	30 mL
to taste	salt and freshly ground black pepper	to taste
½ cup	white wine	125 mL
4 Tbsp	butter	60 mL
1	baguette	1

METHOD

Place the squares of foil on your work surface. Divide the potatoes, onion slices, corn, mussels, and shrimp evenly among the packages.

Season with the chopped parsley, salt, and pepper. Pull up the sides to partially enclose the ingredients. Add 2 Tbsp (30 mL) of wine and 1 Tbsp (15 mL) of butter to each package. Tightly fold the seams to seal the packages well.

Build a fire, and when the flames have died down and the coals are glowing, set a grill over the coals and place the packages on the grill. Cook for 20 minutes or until the vegetables are lightly steamed and the seafood is cooked (the mussels will open and the shrimp will be pink).

To serve, place the packages into bowls, and open each one carefully to release the steam. Serve with a crusty baguette and butter on the side.

This recipe is inspired by the fabulous lobster ragout made at the Elora Mill Country Inn in Ontario, where it is served with handmade mustard spaetzle, tiny noodle-like dumplings. This variation on that theme can be served over rice or fettucine, or spooned into baked puff pastry shells. Makes 4 servings.

LOBSTER SCALLOP RAGOUT

INGREDIENTS

2 lb	uncooked lobster tails	1 kg
½ cup	butter	125 mL
12	medium-sized scallops	12
1½ cups	sliced button mushrooms	375 mL
1 cup	whipping cream (35%)	250 mL
2 tsp	Dijon mustard	10 mL
to taste	salt and freshly ground black pepper	to taste
1½ cups	baby spinach, washed and dried	375 mL

METHOD

Extract the meat from the lobster tails and chop into small pieces. Melt 4 Tbsp (60 mL) of the butter in a large skillet over medium heat. Add the scallops and cook for 45 seconds on each side. Remove and keep warm.

Melt the remaining 4 Tbsp (60 mL) butter and add the lobster meat. Cook until tender, about 3–5 minutes. Remove and keep warm.

Add the mushrooms to the pan and cook until tender, about 5 minutes. Add the cream, mustard, salt and pepper, and combine well. Bring to a boil and then reduce to a simmer and cook until the sauce thickens slightly.

Return the lobster and scallops to the pan and add the spinach. Serve when the lobster and scallops are heated through and the spinach is wilted, about 1 minute.

This seafood stew can be made with any assortment of fresh, frozen, or canned seafood you can get your hands on and is less complicated than cioppino or bouillabaisse. It needs crusty bread to mop up the broth. Serves 4.

SEAFOOD STEW

INGREDIENTS

2 Tbsp	olive oil	30 mL
1	large onion, chopped	1
3	garlic cloves, crushed or chopped	3
1 Tbsp	dried oregano	15 mL
1 tsp	fennel seeds, crushed	5 mL
1	28 oz (796 mL) can diced or crushed tomatoes	1
2 cups	canned clam juice	500 mL
1 cup	dry white wine	250 mL
2	5 oz (142 g) cans clams, drained (reserve the liquid)	2
1 lb	uncooked large shrimp (31/35), peeled and deveined	500 g
1 lb	cod, haddock, or other whitefish fillets, cut into 2-inch (5 cm) pieces	500 g
1	4 oz (120 g) can crabmeat, drained	1
½ cup	chopped fresh basil or parsley	125 mL
to taste	salt and pepper	to taste
to taste	cayenne pepper	to taste

METHOD

Heat the oil in a large pot or Dutch oven set over medium heat. Sauté the onion, garlic, oregano, and fennel seeds for about 8 minutes, until the onion is tender. Add the tomatoes, clam juice, wine, and the reserved liquid from the clams. Bring to a boil, then reduce the heat, and simmer for 20–30 minutes, until slightly thickened.

Add the clams, shrimp, fish, and crabmeat, and simmer for 5 minutes, until the shrimp and fish are opaque. Stir in the basil and season to taste with salt, pepper, and cayenne pepper. Serve.

OPTION

You could also add ½ lb (250 g) bay scallops along with the seafood, or instead of the fish. Try adding the grated zest of an orange and a generous pinch of dried red pepper flakes.

This bouillabaisse has tropical overtones—a meal in itself when you're feeling exotic. It's very rich and creamy, so serve it in shallow bowls over mounds of fragrant basmati rice. For a traditional New Year's treat, instead of cooking the rice in water, cook it with coconut milk, a touch of minced jalapeño pepper, some cooked red beans, and a sprinkle of chopped fresh thyme. Serves 8–10.

ISLAND BOUILLABAISSE

INGREDIENTS

2	medium tart apples, peeled and chopped	2
2	medium bananas, peeled	2
¾ cup	raisins	175 mL
¼ cup	Madras-style curry powder	60 mL
3	garlic cloves, minced	3
½ tsp	ground cumin	2 mL
2 tsp	Worcestershire sauce	10 mL
4 cups	coconut milk	1 L
4 cups	chicken stock	1 L
¼ tsp	crushed saffron threads or turmeric	1 mL
¼ cup	freshly squeezed lemon or lime juice	60 mL
¼ cup	brown sugar	60 mL
1½ cups	whipping cream (35%)	375 mL
1 cup	finely diced red bell peppers	250 mL
1½ lb	cubed snapper, halibut, or other firm white fish	750 g
32	large prawns, peeled and deveined	32
32	sea scallops	32
24	large mussels, scrubbed and debearded	24
½ cup	chopped fresh cilantro	125 mL
4–5 cups	hot, cooked basmati rice	1–1.25 L

METHOD

In a large saucepan, combine the apple, banana, raisins, curry powder, garlic, cumin, Worcestershire, coconut milk, stock, saffron, lemon juice, and brown sugar. Bring to a boil over medium-high heat. Reduce the heat to medium-low, cover, and simmer for 30 minutes. Cool the mixture slightly and purée with a food processor or hand blender until smooth. Add the cream and whirl to combine. (You can make this portion of the soup a day in advance. Simply refrigerate until you are ready to fin-ish before serving.)

Reheat the soup base over medium heat in a deep Dutch oven or wok. When it boils, add the red peppers and cubed fish. Simmer for 5 minutes. Add the prawns, scallops, and mussels. Cover the pot and raise the heat to medium-high. Simmer for 3–5 minutes or until the shrimp are pink and the mussels are open.

Discard any mussels that don't open and stir in half the cilantro.

To serve, mound ½ cup (125 mL) of rice in the center of 8 shallow soup plates (you can press the rice into a small ramekin or custard cup and unmold in the middle of the bowl to make it look more professional).

Surround the rice with the seafood and ladle the soup overtop. Sprinkle with the reserved cilantro and serve.

Also referred to in my kitchen as a dish for consenting adults, this is a gloriously messy enterprise, fun to make with more than two hands on deck and definitely not meant as a prelude to any sort of new-romance liaison. In fact, it's a good dinner prelude to a brisk nap. You can begin this a day ahead if you stop prep just before adding the seafood. Serves 4–6.

THE LOVERS' CIOPPINO

INGREDIENTS

¼ cup	olive oil	60 mL
5	onions, chopped chunky	5
lots	chopped garlic	lots
3	red peppers, seeded and chopped	3
2	green peppers, seeded and chopped	2
5	celery stalks with leaves, chopped	5
1	bulb fresh fennel (with fronds), chopped	1
3	medium zucchini, chopped into big chunks	3
1	bottle Zinfandel (get a good, hearty one)	1
8 cups	fish stock (or vegetable stock)	2 L
2 lb	ripe Roma tomatoes, chopped	1 kg
10	fresh basil leaves, chopped	10
1 tsp	fennel seeds	5 mL
3	bay leaves	3
to taste	red pepper flakes (optional)	to taste
to taste	salt and pepper	to taste
3	slices white bread	3
2	jalapeño peppers, seeded and chopped	2
	more garlic, to taste	
½ cup	olive oil	125 mL
12	clams, cleaned	12
12	mussels, cleaned	12
12	prawns (or more)	12
1	whole crab, disassembled	1
1	bunch fresh parsley, chopped	1
1 lb	halibut fillet, cut into chunks	500 g
¾ cup	olive oil	175 mL
24	very thin baguette slices, toasted and rubbed with garlic	24

METHOD

Heat ¼ cup (60 mL) olive oil in a deep pan or wok. Add the onions and garlic and cook 10 minutes on low heat until the onions are soft but not browned. Add the peppers, celery, fennel, and zucchini and cook 10 minutes more.

Transfer everything to a big warm stew or soup pot. Pour in the bottle of Zinfandel . . . yes, all of it. Pour in about the same amount of fish stock, but reserve a few spoonfuls for the baguette spread. Add the tomatoes, then the basil, fennel, bay leaves, red pepper flakes, and salt and pepper. Stir well, turn up the heat, and let it bubble once it's come to the boil. Simmer, partly covered, for 20 minutes. Adjust seasonings.

Soak the white bread slices in a little water and squeeze dry. Using a mortar and pestle, pound the bread and jalapeños and some garlic together into a paste. Add ½ cup (125 mL) oil, a small trickle at a time (as if you are making mayo) and keep pounding. Add a few spoonfuls of the reserved fish stock and some salt and pepper. Set aside.

Bring the cioppino to another boil and add the clams, mussels, prawns, and crab. Add lots of chopped parsley. Adjust the liquid (stock and wine) as needed. Cover and simmer until the clams and mussels open. Add the halibut and cook another 3 minutes or so until the halibut is cooked through.

Take the cioppino off the heat, collect yourself, and set the pot before the dinner group. Serve the toasted baguette slices with the garlic-oil-pepper spread you pounded in the mortar. You can also put one in the bottom of a bowl and pour the stew all over it. Roll up your sleeves and get down and messy. Drink lots more Zinfandel—starting with white if you like, moving through the lighter style, and ending with one of those old vines numbers.

Every Cajun cook makes gumbo—and every gumbo is unique. Classic versions are loaded with shrimp, sausage, chicken, and even wild game ('gator anyone?). I like this simplified combo of chicken, shrimp, spicy sausage, and sweet peppers. Beer—the secret ingredient in this gumbo—is the perfect beverage to consume with it, too. Serves 6.

CHICKEN, SHRIMP & SAUSAGE GUMBO

INGREDIENTS

2 tsp	salt	10 mL
2 tsp	garlic powder	10 mL
1 tsp	dried thyme	5 mL
1 tsp	cayenne	5 mL
2 lb	boneless, skinless chicken thighs	1 kg
½ cup	all-purpose flour	125 mL
4 Tbsp	olive oil	60 mL
1	large onion, chopped	1
2	celery stalks, chopped	2
3	garlic cloves, chopped	3
1	yellow bell pepper, seeded and chopped	1
1	red bell pepper, seeded and chopped	1
1	4 oz (125 g) spicy sausage, sliced	1
1	14 oz (398 mL) can tomatoes, puréed in a food processor or blender	1
1	12 oz (355 mL) bottle dark beer	1
1 cup	chicken broth or water	250 mL
1 Tbsp	Worcestershire sauce	15 mL
2	bay leaves	2
2 tsp	ground marjoram	10 mL
1 lb	large shrimp, peeled and deveined	500 g
to taste	salt and freshly ground black pepper	to taste
for six	steamed long-grain rice	for six

Recipe continues on the next page . . .

METHOD

In a small bowl, mix together the salt, garlic powder, thyme, and cayenne. Set aside.

Cut the chicken into 2-inch (5 cm) chunks and place in a bowl. Rub the chicken pieces with 2 tsp (10 mL) of the spice mixture and marinate it in the refrigerator for 20 minutes.

Put the remaining spice mixture and the flour into a large, zippered plastic bag. When the chicken pieces have marinated, add them to the bag, seal, and shake to coat well with the seasoned flour.

In a large heavy pot or Dutch oven, heat 2 Tbsp (30 mL) of the oil over medium-high heat. Remove the chicken from the bag, reserving the flour, and sauté the chicken pieces in batches until they are nicely browned. Remove the chicken from the pan and set aside.

Reduce the heat to medium-low and add the remaining 2 Tbsp (30 mL) of the olive oil to the pan. Add the reserved spice flour to the oil and stir to form a roux

(add a little more oil if the mixture seems too dry). Cook the roux over medium heat, stirring frequently, until it turns the color of peanut butter. Stir carefully; roux is very hot and can burn your skin.

Add the onion, celery, garlic, bell peppers, and sausage to the pan. Keep the heat fairly high, and sauté, stirring occasionally, for 5 minutes. Add the puréed tomatoes, beer, chicken broth, Worcestershire, bay leaves, marjoram, and the browned chicken to the pot.

Bring to a boil over medium-high heat, then reduce the heat to low and cover. Simmer for 45–60 minutes until the chicken is tender.

Add the shrimp, cover the pot, and simmer for 5 minutes or until the shrimp curl and turn pink. Season to taste with salt and pepper. Mound some steamed rice in each of six individual soup plates and the ladle the gumbo around the rice.

Oftentimes, when I see paella on a restaurant menu, I get very excited—only to find that what I'm served bears no resemblance to the traditional dish I love so much. Use only short-grain rice; long-grain varieties produce dishes entirely different in character, flavor, and texture. The traditional rice to use is Bomba, but it can be difficult to track down. Try using a risotto rice, such as Carnaroli or Arborio, instead. *Serves 8–10.*

PAELLA

INGREDIENTS

6 cups	strong chicken broth	1.5 L		¼ cup	chorizo, cooked and cut into ¼-inch (6 mm) pieces	60 mL
3	big pinches saffron	3		1 lb	small shrimp	500 g
1	small onion, whole	1		18	clams	18
1	chicken breast	1		18	mussels	18
½ cup	extra virgin olive oil	125 mL				
1	small onion, chopped	1				
4	green onions, chopped	4				
4	garlic cloves, minced	4				
2	piquillo peppers or other roasted red pepper, chopped	2				
¼ cup	diced cured ham	60 mL				
3 cups	Bomba or short-grain rice	750 mL				
5 Tbsp	chopped fresh parsley	75 mL				
2	bay leaves, crumbled	2				
½ cup	dry white wine	125 mL				
1 Tbsp	lemon juice	15 mL				
to taste	kosher salt	to taste				

Recipe continues on the next page . . .

METHOD

Preheat the oven to 350°F (180°C).

Place the broth, saffron, and whole onion in a saucepan over medium heat. Cover and simmer for 15 minutes. Remove the onion and measure the broth. You will need exactly 5½ cups (1.4 L). If you have less, add water to make up the difference.

While the broth is simmering, bake the chicken in a roasting pan in the oven until almost cooked through, about 20 minutes. Allow to cool slightly and cut into large chunks.

In a paella pan or large, shallow, flat-bottomed pan, heat the olive oil over high heat. Reduce the heat slightly and add the chopped onion, green onions, garlic, and peppers. Sauté until the onion is wilted. Mix in the diced ham and rice. Stir to coat the rice with the oil. Sprinkle in the chopped parsley and the bay leaves.

Stir in the reserved broth, which should be boiling hot, then the wine and lemon juice. Season with salt.

Bring to a boil and cook, uncovered and stirring every so often, over medium heat for about 7 minutes, or until the rice is no longer soupy but some liquid remains. Add the chunks of cooked chicken, chorizo, and shrimp. Push the clams and mussels into the rice, with the edge that will open facing up. Bake, uncovered, at 325°F (160°C) for about 20 minutes or until the mussels and clams have opened. Remove from the oven and let sit lightly covered with foil, for about 10 minutes. Serve.

If you purchase unpeeled raw seafood, be sure to save the shells—they're full of flavor! Simply place them in the freezer (they are quite compact) until you have enough to use. You can use just one kind of shell, or a combination of them. Makes 8 cups (2 L).

SHELLFISH STOCK

INGREDIENTS

2 Tbsp	vegetable oil	30 mL
4½ lb	mixed seafood shells (prawn, crab, and lobster)	2 kg
1 cup	white wine	250 mL
7 cups	cold water	1.75 L
2	onions, peeled and chopped	2
1	celery rib, chopped	1
1	tomato, chopped	1
1	fresh thyme sprig	1
1	bay leaf	1
2	parsley stems	2
1	lemon, cut in half	1

METHOD

In a medium stockpot, heat the oil over medium heat and sauté the shells until they are pink, about 4–6 minutes. Cover with the white wine and water. Bring to a simmer gradually, skimming and discarding any impurities that rise to the surface.

Once the stock is at a simmer, add the remaining ingredients. Continue to simmer for 20 minutes. Strain and reserve the liquid. Refrigerate or freeze until ready to use.

INDEX